First World War

and Army of Occupation

War Diary

France, Belgium and Germany

37 DIVISION
Headquarters, Branches and Services
Royal Army Veterinary Corps
Assistant Director Veterinary Services
5 May 1915 - 21 April 1919

WO95/2520/2

The Naval & Military Press Ltd
www.nmarchive.com
Published in association with The National Archives

Published by

The Naval & Military Press Ltd

Unit 10 Ridgewood Industrial Park,
Uckfield, East Sussex,
TN22 5QE England
Tel: +44 (0) 1825 749494

www.naval-military-press.com
www.nmarchive.com

This diary has been reprinted in facsimile from the original. Any imperfections are inevitably reproduced and the quality may fall short of modern type and cartographic standards.

Contents

Document type	Place/Title	Date From	Date To
Heading	WO95/2520/2		
Heading	37th Division A.D.V.S. May 1915-Apr 1919		
Heading	37th Division H.Q. 37th Division A.D.V.S. Vol.I May June July & August 15		
War Diary	Salisbury	05/05/1915	05/05/1915
War Diary	Chamberlain	06/05/1915	30/07/1915
War Diary	Tilques	31/07/1915	04/08/1915
War Diary	Renescure	04/08/1915	04/08/1915
War Diary	Caestre	05/08/1915	25/08/1915
War Diary	Doullens	25/08/1915	31/08/1915
Heading	37th Division H.Q. 37th Division A.D.V.S. Vol:2 Sept 15		
War Diary	Pas	29/09/1915	30/09/1915
War Diary	Pas	26/09/1915	28/09/1915
War Diary	Pas	22/09/1915	25/09/1915
War Diary	Pas	18/09/1915	21/09/1915
War Diary	Pas	14/09/1915	17/09/1915
War Diary	Pas	10/09/1915	13/09/1915
War Diary	Doullens	04/09/1915	05/09/1915
War Diary	Pas	06/09/1915	09/09/1915
War Diary	Doullens	01/09/1915	03/09/1915
Heading	H.Q. 37th Div: A.D.V.S. Vol 3 Oct 15		
War Diary	Pas	26/10/1915	31/10/1915
War Diary	Pas	20/10/1915	25/10/1915
War Diary	Pas	17/10/1915	20/10/1915
War Diary	Pas	10/10/1915	16/10/1915
War Diary	Pas	04/10/1915	09/10/1915
War Diary	Pas	01/10/1915	04/10/1915
Heading	H.Q. 37th Div A.D.V.S. Vol:4 Nov 15		
War Diary	Pas	25/11/1915	01/12/1915
War Diary	Pas	20/11/1915	24/11/1915
War Diary	Pas	14/11/1915	19/11/1915
War Diary	Pas	07/11/1915	13/11/1915
War Diary	Pas	01/11/1915	06/11/1915
Heading	A.D.V.S. 37th Div. Vol:5		
War Diary	Pas	21/12/1915	31/12/1915
War Diary	Pas	11/12/1915	20/12/1915
War Diary	Pas	01/12/1915	10/12/1915
Heading	A.D.V.S. 37th Div Vol: 6		
War Diary	Pas	30/01/1916	31/01/1916
War Diary	Pas	24/01/1916	29/01/1916
War Diary	Pas	17/01/1916	23/01/1916
War Diary	Pas	09/01/1916	16/01/1916
War Diary	Pas	01/01/1916	08/01/1916
Heading	A.D.V.S. 37th Div Vol: 7		
War Diary	Pas	19/02/1916	21/02/1916
War Diary	Bavincourt	22/02/1916	29/02/1916
War Diary	Pas	11/02/1916	19/02/1916
War Diary	Pas	04/02/1916	10/02/1916
War Diary	Pas	01/02/1916	03/02/1916

Heading	ADVS 37th Div Vol 8		
War Diary	Bavincourt	01/03/1916	20/03/1916
War Diary	Lucheux	21/03/1916	30/04/1916
War Diary	Lucheux	25/04/1916	27/04/1916
War Diary	Lucheux	19/04/1916	24/04/1916
War Diary	Lucheux	10/04/1916	18/04/1916
War Diary	Lucheux	01/04/1916	09/04/1916
War Diary	Bavincourt	26/05/1916	31/05/1916
War Diary	Bavincourt	14/05/1916	25/05/1916
War Diary	Bavincourt	06/05/1916	13/05/1916
War Diary	Lucheux	01/05/1916	03/05/1916
War Diary	Bavincourt	05/05/1916	30/06/1916
War Diary	Bavincourt	13/06/1916	25/06/1916
War Diary	Bavincourt	01/06/1916	12/06/1916
War Diary	Bavincourt	01/07/1916	04/07/1916
War Diary	Pas	05/07/1916	08/07/1916
War Diary	Bryas	18/07/1916	19/07/1916
War Diary	Legomte	20/07/1916	26/07/1916
War Diary	Pas	09/07/1916	15/07/1916
War Diary	Liencourt	16/07/1916	16/07/1916
War Diary	Bryas	17/07/1916	17/07/1916
War Diary	Le Comte	27/07/1916	28/07/1916
War Diary	Camblain L'Abbe	29/07/1916	15/08/1916
War Diary	Bruay	15/08/1916	31/08/1916
Heading	War Diary Sept 1916 A.D.V.S. 37th Divn Vol 14		
War Diary	Bruay	01/09/1916	18/09/1916
War Diary	Barlin	19/09/1916	18/10/1916
War Diary	Ruellecourt	19/10/1916	20/10/1916
War Diary	Le Cauroy	21/10/1916	21/10/1916
War Diary	Marieux	22/10/1916	15/11/1916
War Diary	Hedauville	16/11/1916	16/11/1916
War Diary	Forceville	16/11/1916	24/11/1916
War Diary	Marieux	25/11/1916	13/12/1916
War Diary	Frohen-Le-Grand	14/12/1916	14/12/1916
War Diary	Fletrs	15/12/1916	15/12/1916
War Diary	Monchy-Cayeux	16/12/1916	16/12/1916
War Diary	Norrentes-Fontes	17/12/1916	17/12/1916
War Diary	Stvenant	18/12/1916	21/12/1916
War Diary	Lestrem	21/12/1916	31/01/1917
Heading	War Diary A.D.V.S. 37th Divn Feb 1917 Vol 19		
War Diary	Lestrem	01/02/1917	13/02/1917
War Diary	Braquemont	14/02/1917	28/02/1917
Heading	War Diary A.D.V.S. 37th Divn March 1917 Vol 20		
War Diary	Braquemont	01/03/1917	03/03/1917
War Diary	Norrent-Fontes	04/03/1917	09/03/1917
War Diary	Roellecourt	10/03/1917	31/03/1917
Heading	War Diary A.D.V.S. 37th Divn Apl 1917 Vol 21		
War Diary	Roellecourt	01/04/1917	05/04/1917
War Diary	Agnez	06/04/1917	13/04/1917
War Diary	Lignereuil	14/04/1917	21/04/1917
War Diary	Etrun	22/04/1917	25/04/1917
War Diary	Arras	26/04/1917	29/04/1917
War Diary	Lignereuil	30/04/1917	18/05/1917
War Diary	Warlus	19/05/1917	20/05/1917
War Diary	Warlus Arras	21/05/1917	21/05/1917
War Diary	Arras	22/05/1917	31/05/1917

Heading	War Diary A.D.V.S. 37th Division June 1917 Vol 23		
War Diary	Arras	01/06/1917	01/06/1917
War Diary	Lignereuil	02/06/1917	07/06/1917
War Diary	Bomy	08/06/1917	23/06/1917
War Diary	Steenbecque	24/06/1917	24/06/1917
War Diary	Locre	25/06/1917	29/06/1917
War Diary	Dranoutre	30/06/1917	30/06/1917
Heading	War Diary D.A.D.V.S 37th Divn July 1917 Vol 24		
War Diary	Dranoutre	01/07/1917	31/07/1917
Heading	War Diary D.A.D.V.S. 37th Divn Aug 1917 Vol 25		
War Diary	Dranoutre	01/08/1917	07/08/1917
War Diary	Scherpenburg	08/08/1917	31/08/1917
Heading	War Diary D.ADV.S. 37th Divn Sept 1917 Vol 26		
War Diary	Scherpenburg	01/09/1917	11/09/1917
War Diary	St. Jans Cappel	12/09/1917	28/09/1917
War Diary	Zevecoten	29/09/1917	30/09/1917
Heading	War Diary D.A.D.V.S. 37th Division Oct 1917 Vol 27		
War Diary	Dezon Camp	01/10/1917	14/10/1917
War Diary	Dezon	16/10/1917	16/10/1917
War Diary	St Jan Capel	17/10/1917	09/11/1917
War Diary	Scherpenberg	10/11/1917	12/01/1918
War Diary	Blaringhem	13/01/1918	17/02/1918
War Diary	Westoutre	18/02/1918	24/02/1918
War Diary	Anzac Camp	25/02/1918	28/02/1918
War Diary	Anzac Camp between	01/03/1918	01/03/1918
War Diary	Biekebusch	02/03/1918	02/03/1918
War Diary	Ypres	03/03/1918	26/03/1918
War Diary	Anzac Camp	27/03/1918	27/03/1918
War Diary	Pas	31/03/1918	02/04/1918
War Diary	Couin	03/04/1918	15/04/1918
War Diary	Authie	16/04/1918	23/04/1918
War Diary	Henu	24/04/1918	16/05/1918
War Diary	Authie	17/05/1918	05/06/1918
War Diary	Cavillon	06/06/1918	09/06/1918
War Diary	Wailly	10/06/1918	20/06/1918
War Diary	Pas	21/06/1918	31/07/1918
Miscellaneous	On His Majesty's Service. D.A.G. 3rd Echelon G.H.Q.		
Miscellaneous			
War Diary	Henu	01/08/1918	25/08/1918
War Diary	Fonquevillers	26/08/1918	31/08/1918
War Diary	Achiet-Le-Grand	01/09/1918	08/09/1918
War Diary	Favreuil	09/09/1918	11/09/1918
War Diary	J 36 D 9.1 Ref. Map 57 C.	12/09/1918	15/09/1918
War Diary	J 6d. 9.1	16/09/1918	19/09/1918
War Diary	Velu	20/09/1918	20/09/1918
War Diary	Achiet Le Grand	21/09/1918	29/09/1918
War Diary	Villiers Au Flos	30/09/1918	30/09/1918
War Diary	Havrincourt Wood (P18d) Sheet 57.c)	01/10/1918	06/10/1918
War Diary	Q 29 Central Sheet 57c	07/10/1918	07/10/1918
War Diary	Q 29 Central	08/10/1918	09/10/1918
War Diary	Haucourt	10/10/1918	24/10/1918
War Diary	Briastre	25/10/1918	05/11/1918
War Diary	Neuville	06/11/1918	10/11/1918
War Diary	Caudry	11/11/1918	02/12/1918
War Diary	Gommegnies	03/12/1918	14/12/1918
War Diary	Sous Le Bois	15/12/1918	19/12/1918

War Diary Gosselies 20/12/1918 21/04/1919

37TH DIVISION

A. D. V. S.

MAY ~~AUG~~ 1915-APR 1919

37th Division

21/6874

HQ. 37th Division
A.D.V.S.

Vol: I

May June July & August 15

Apr '19

Instructions regarding War Diaries and Intelligence Summaries are contained in F. S. Regs., Part II. and the Staff Manual respectively. Title pages will be prepared in manuscript.

WAR DIARY
or
INTELLIGENCE SUMMARY.
(Erase heading not required.)

Army Form C. 2118.

Place	Date	Hour	Summary of Events and Information	Remarks and references to Appendices
Salisbury.	5 5/15	3 P.M.	Reported arrival from France to D.D.V.S. Southern Command. to take over duties of A.D.V.S. 37th Division –	
Chadderton.	6 5/15	9.30 A.M.	Reported my arrival at Head Qrs of the Division at Chadderton. Had an interview with the G.O.C. and met all the other Officers on the Head Qrs Staff. and took up my duties forthwith. Going into residence at Chadderton House on the same day –	
"	7 5/15		Had an interview with my Veterinary Officers. six of whom have already arrived and been posted to duties for time as follows.	
			Lieut A. A. Pryer. VC 28th Mobile Veterinary Section (which has already arrived).	
			" Gilland. V.O. G. 123rd 126th Bdes and 37th Divisional Ammunition Column R.A.	
			" Huston " " 111th Infantry, Brigade – + 37th Divisional Train –	
			" Stanford " " 124th + 125th Bdes R.A.	
			" Waddell " " 110th Infantry Brigade.	
			" Tully-Christie " " 112 " " (This Officer is suffering from a severe injury of the left arm & does not look like doing much work)	
			with the exception of Lt Pryer and Gilland who have already had several months active service experience. the others are very inexperienced as to their duties –	
"	8 5/15		Began a series of regular daily rounds of inspecting sick animals – animals for casting.	

1577 Wt. W10791/1773 500,000 1/15 D. D. & L. A.D.S.S./Forms/C. 2118.

Army Form C. 2118.

Instructions regarding War Diaries and Intelligence Summaries are contained in F. S. Regs., Part II. and the Staff Manual respectively. Title pages will be prepared in manuscript.

WAR DIARY
or
INTELLIGENCE SUMMARY.
(Erase heading not required.)

Place	Date	Hour	Summary of Events and Information	Remarks and references to Appendices
Cholderton	8/5/15		(Continued) and instructing my Veterinary Officers. In the afternoon visited the D.D.V.S. Southern Command and reported progress.	
"	9/5/15		Supplied all my V.O's with a copy of Regulations for A.V. Services, Standing Orders for the A.V.C. Army Forms &c and consulted with them on several points.	
"	10/5/15		Spent most of the day in my office, and issued some detailed instructions to all V.O's of the Division.	
"	12/5/15		To Salisbury and had an interview with the D.A.D.R. Southern Command and arranged to co-operate with him in all matters concerning the animals of my Division and to assist in the ~~making~~ preventing wastage, and unnecessary correspondence. Lieut Tully-Christie placed on the Sick List this day suffering from Fracture left arm	
"	13/5/15 }		Nothing particular to record. except that I drew a charger for myself from the Remount Depot	
"	19/5/15 }		Salisbury on the 18th inst.	
"	20/5/15		Lieut Payne placed on the Sick List. Lieut Gillard placed in temporary command of the Mobile Vety Hospital in addition to his other duties.	
"	22/5/15		Corporal Simkiss A.V.C. arrived as Clerk.	
"	23/5/15		Spent most of the day instructing my clerk in his duties.	

1577 Wt. W10791/1773 500,000 1/15 D. D. & L. A.D.S.S./Forms/C. 2118.

Army Form C. 2118.

Instructions regarding War Diaries and Intelligence Summaries are contained in F. S. Regs., Part II. and the Staff Manual respectively. Title pages will be prepared in manuscript.

WAR DIARY
or
INTELLIGENCE SUMMARY.
(Erase heading not required.)

Place	Date	Hour	Summary of Events and Information	Remarks and references to Appendices
Cholderton	24/5/15		Reported by wire to Officer i/c Records that Corporal supplied to me as a clerk is useless as such.	
"	26/5/15		Corporal McAlister arrived from Woolwich as clerk vice Simkins who was returned to the Depot forthwith.	
"	27/5/15		Visited Lieut Payne in Hospital again and found out that he had had a slight relapse.	
"	28/5/15		Spent most of the day instructing Lieut Gilland in office work and the duties of an O.C. Mobile Vety Section.	
"	29/5/15 }			
"	31/5/15 }		Nothing particular to report.	
			W. A. Pallin Vety Major A.D.V.S. 37th Division	

1577 Wt. W10791/1773 500,000 1/15 D. D. & L. A.D.S.S./Forms/C. 2118.

Instructions regarding War Diaries and Intelligence Summaries are contained in F. S. Regs., Part II. and the Staff Manual respectively. Title pages will be prepared in manuscript.

WAR DIARY
or
INTELLIGENCE SUMMARY.
(Erase heading not required.)

Army Form C. 2118.

Place	Date	Hour	Summary of Events and Information	Remarks and references to Appendices
Cholderton.	1/6/15		Heavy Draught Horses which have been recently issued to the 37th Divisional Train are suffering from Catarrh with complication of Strangles, Contagious Pneumonia & Purpura to rather an alarming extent. Spent the whole morning out at their Camp arranging about their isolation and treatment and necessary steps to prevent the spread of the disease –	
"	3/6/15		To Salisbury to see the D.D.V.S. Southern Command and consult with him regarding Veterinary arrangements for R.A. proceeding to Okehampton Practice Camp. and he agreed to employ Mr Dundas C.V.S. (Civilian) to assist Lt Stafford whom I was sending in Vety charge – also consulted D.D.V.S. regarding the outbreak of Catarrh in the 37th Divisional Train –	
"	4/6/15 – 8/6/15		Nothing particular to report – except that I have busy with Monthly Returns for May – which I did not get completed until the 8th inst –	
"	9/6/15		Visit to Marlborough to see A.D.V.S. 15th Division –	
"	10/6/15		Returned from Marlborough –	
"	11/6/15		Began weekly examination of N.C.O.'s & men of the Mobile Vety Section in Standard I. Afternoon to London for 2 days leave – Lt Gillard acting A.D.V.S. during my absence –	

1577 Wt. W10791/1773 500,000 1/15 D. D. & L. A.D.S.S./Forms/C. 2118.

Instructions regarding War Diaries and Intelligence Summaries are contained in F. S. Regs., Part II. and the Staff Manual respectively. Title pages will be prepared in manuscript.

WAR DIARY
or
INTELLIGENCE SUMMARY.
(Erase heading not required.)

Army Form C. 2118.

Place	Date	Hour	Summary of Events and Information	Remarks and references to Appendices
Chiseldon	13/6/15		Returned from London.	
"	15/6/15		Lieut. T. M. White A.V.C. arrived last night to replace Lieut. Tully Christie whose sick leave has been extended – interviewed him and placed him in charge of the 126th Brigade R.F.A. and the 37th Divisional Ammunition Column.	
"	16/6/15		Lieut. Pryer returned from sick leave and resumed command of the Mobile Vety Section – went through a number of points with him. and also interviewed Mr. Bagley C.V.S. who came over to Tidworth Pennings to supervise the work of Mr Hayden – who has been lent to the Division to give a course of instruction to Farriers. Shoeing smiths etc. etc.	
"	18/6/15		Obtained 9 days leave and proceeded to Ireland via London this afternoon – leaving Lieut Pryer acting A.D.V.S. during my absence.	
"	28/6/15		Returned from Ireland early this morning – to find that 33rd Reserve Park have now got a very considerable number of cases of Catarrh. similar to the 37th Divisional Train amongst their Remounts which have been rapidly arriving during the last 2 weeks. so transferred Lieut Waddell to them as a temporary measure so as to have a V.O on the spot. and inspected the unit carefully myself.	
"	30/6/15		Nothing particular to report.	W. A. Pallin Vety Major A.D.V.S. 37th Division

1577 Wt. W10791/1773 500,000 1/15 D. D. & L. A.D.S.S./Forms/C. 2118.

Instructions regarding War Diaries and Intelligence Summaries are contained in F. S. Regs., Part II. and the Staff Manual respectively. Title pages will be prepared in manuscript.

WAR DIARY
or
INTELLIGENCE SUMMARY.
(Erase heading not required.)

Army Form C. 2118.

Place	Date	Hour	Summary of Events and Information	Remarks and references to Appendices
Cholderton.	1/7/15		A report has been received that a case of Glanders has been found amongst some mules at Hightbridge. So inspected the 37th Divisional Ammunition Column Mules carefully this day as they have recently received a certain number of mules from Highbridge – a number of cases of Catarrh were isolated, but nothing suspicious of Glanders noticed. However all precautions will be taken and a very careful watch kept on these animals –	
"			Arranged to carry out a thorough inspection of every animal in the Division beginning with the 123rd Bde R.A. tomorrow morning –	
"	2/7/15		Inspection of the 123rd Bde. R.A. 10.30 AM to 1 p.M. and 2 pm to 6 p.M.	
"	3/7/15		Examination of N.C.Os: [illegible] of the Mobile Vety Section in Appendix I (Weekly Exam). Case of Psoroptic Mange in 33rd Reserve Park verified and dispatched to Bulford –	
"	4/7/15		Inspection of 33rd Reserve Park for Mange – 5 suspicious cases and 11 contacts isolated and scrapings sent to Aldershot Vety. School for examination.	
"	5/7/15		Morning Inspection of 123rd + 124th Bde R A Veterinary Cases for Casting. Afternoon – Office –	
"	6/7/15		Divisional Route March –	
"	7/7/15		Inspection of the 124 Bde R.A. 10.30 AM to 1 p.M. and 2 p.M to 6 p.M. Special Report to Brigade Major + Chief of the Staff about the poor condition of the horses in 124 Bde Ammunition Column –	

1577 Wt. W10791/1773 500,000 1/15 D. D. & L. A.D.S.S./Forms/C. 2118.

Army Form C. 2118.

Instructions regarding War Diaries and Intelligence Summaries are contained in F. S. Regs., Part II. and the Staff Manual respectively. Title pages will be prepared in manuscript.

WAR DIARY
or
INTELLIGENCE SUMMARY.
(Erase heading not required.)

Place	Date	Hour	Summary of Events and Information	Remarks and references to Appendices
Chiseldon.	8/7/15		Inspection 126th Bde R.A. 10.30 AM to 1 P.M and 2 P.M to 6 P.M. Isolated 1 suspicious case of Mange from A. Battery 126 Bde R.A.	126 Bde R.A.
"	10/7/15	10.30 AM	Weekly Examination of N.C.O's & men of the Mobile Vety Section.	
		11.30 AM.	Inspection of 125th & 126th Bde R.A. Veterinary Cases for casting – Afternoon to Salisbury –	
"	11/7/15		Sunday – Morning Office –	
"	12/7/15	10.30 AM	Mobilization Parade of the 28th Mobile Veterinary Section. Checked all their Equipment &c and made them do a short Route March. Afternoon – Inspected 110th 111th & 112th Infantry Brigade Veterinary Cases for casting –	
"	13/7/15	10.30 AM	Inspection of the 37th Divisional Ammunition Column 10.30 AM to 1 P.M and 2 P.M to 6 P.M. Report from Aldershot Vety School that case of suspected Mange in A Battery 126 Bde is Sarcoptic Mange –	
"	14/7/15	10 AM	Had a meeting of all my V.O.'s at Tidworth Pennings to inspect the case of Sarcoptic Mange previous to its departure to Bulford. And while there the V.O. of 126 Bde R.A brought to my notice an animal belonging to D Battery of that Brigade with suspicious symptoms of Epizootic Lymphangitis which I also had sent to Bulford after a smear had been taken from one of the nodules – Necessary instructions given & precautions adopted –	
"	"	10.30 AM	Inspected the 125th Bde. 10.30 AM to 1 PM + 2 PM to 6 PM.	

1577 Wt. W10791/1773 500,000 1/15 D. D. & L. A.D.S.S./Forms/C. 2118.

Army Form C. 2118.

Instructions regarding War Diaries and Intelligence Summaries are contained in F. S. Regs., Part II. and the Staff Manual respectively. Title pages will be prepared in manuscript.

WAR DIARY
or
INTELLIGENCE SUMMARY.
(Erase heading not required.)

Place	Date	Hour	Summary of Events and Information	Remarks and references to Appendices
Cholderton.	15.7.15	10.30 AM	Inspection of the 37th Divisional Train – 10.30 AM to 1 PM and 2 PM to 5 PM. Returned at 5.30 PM to find that D.D.V.S. had been wiring and telephoning about the suspected case of Epizootic Lymphangitis sent to Bulford yesterday – wired full particulars to him and also sent a written report by special messenger.	
	16.7.15	11.30 AM	Re-inspected A & B Batteries 126th Bde R.A. the former for Mange and the latter for Epizootic Lymphangitis. No more suspicious cases of either – Afternoon. Completed Inspection of the 37th Divisional Train. As a large number of animals were away yesterday and therefore could not be seen – outbreak of Catarrh has now subsided and those animals which were debilitated from the disease are picking up rapidly – but there is a good deal of Ringworm which is being thoroughly dealt with – wire from Aldershot saying examination of pus from suspicious case is Negative –	
	17.7.15	10.30 AM	Inspection of the Royal Engineers Signal Company + 3 Field Companies 10.30 AM to 1 PM. Afternoon. Weekly Inspection of the N.C.O.s' horses of the Mobile Vety. Section in Appendix I	
	18.7.15		Sunday.	
	19.7.15		Inspected all the cases in the Mobile Vety. Section – noting those animals for discharge, transfer to Bulford + doubtful cases for further inspection.	

1577 Wt. W10791/1773 500,000 1/15 D. D. & L. A.D.S.S./Forms/C. 2118.

Instructions regarding War Diaries and Intelligence Summaries are contained in F. S. Regs., Part II. and the Staff Manual respectively. Title pages will be prepared in manuscript.

WAR DIARY
or
INTELLIGENCE SUMMARY.
(Erase heading not required.)

Army Form C. 2118.

Place	Date	Hour	Summary of Events and Information	Remarks and references to Appendices
Chiseldon	20/7/15	10 AM	Inspection of the 110th Infantry Brigade –	
		2 PM	" " " 111th " "	
"	21/7/15	10 AM to 6 PM	Assisted in examination with Mr. Bazley C.V.S. Division – of the Shoeing Smiths and Cold Shoers trained by Mr Hayden – The Wiltshire County Council Farrier which the Division have had employed holding classes of instruction in Farriery during the last 2 months.	
	22/7/15		Completed examination of Shoeing Smiths – in the morning – Afternoon Office –	
	23/7/15		Inspected all the cases in the Mobile Vety Section and noted those fit for service or for transfer to Bulford. Late in the afternoon had another Epizootic case. Owing to a badly worded wire from Commandant A.V. School, Aldershot – Held up all the arrangements for clearing the Mobile Vety Section and stopped all movements of animals in and out of the Section and 33rd Remount Park from which unit the suspected case came. Visited the 33rd Remount Park – and had the case along with another rather suspicious case sent to Bulford – and sent full report to D.D.V.S. Southern Command by special messenger.	
	24/7/15		Epizootic lymphangitis cases off – Inspected Remount Park in the morning. R.A.M.C. in the afternoon and went into Salisbury to interview D.D.V.S. S.C.	

1577 Wt. W10791/1773 500,000 1/15 D. D. & L. A.D.S.S./Forms/C. 2118.

Instructions regarding War Diaries and Intelligence Summaries are contained in F. S. Regs., Part II. and the Staff Manual respectively. Title pages will be prepared in manuscript.

WAR DIARY
or
INTELLIGENCE SUMMARY.
(Erase heading not required.)

Army Form C. 2118

Place	Date	Hour	Summary of Events and Information	Remarks and references to Appendices
Cholderton	25.7.15		Sunday – To London for the day – Lieut Pryce acting for me during my absence.	
"	26.7.15	9 AM	Inspection of the 112th Infantry & Pioneer Battalion – Officers Yorkshire Dragoons – Issued orders to all Vety Officers for the move of the Division.	
"	27.7.15		Rode round all the Camps, ~~and~~ saw each Vety Officer and made final arrangements for the disposal of all cases.	
			Interview with Major Burnett Assistant D.D.V.S. Southern Command informed him of all my arrangements – Office work up to midnight –	
"	28.7.15		Finished off all my office work ~~at~~ and left Cholderton at 10 AM for Tidworth from where I departed at 11.20 AM with the Head Qrs Transport and animals – which arrived Southampton ~~Docks~~ at 12.15 p.m embarked on City of Dunkirk at sailed at 4.30 p.m. The following were the units and number of animals on Board.	
			4th Field Ambulance ~~[illegible]~~ 27 — 110th Inf Bde. H Qrs 31	
			8th Leicesters 73 — No 2 Signal Co. 8	
			A/123 Bde R.A. 66 — 2 P.G. Co. A.S.C. 31	
			37th D. H Qrs. 48 — Total = 306	
			" Div R.A. H.Q 22	

1577 Wt. W10791/1773 500,000 1/15 D. D. & L. A.D.S.S./Forms/C. 2118.

Instructions regarding War Diaries and Intelligence Summaries are contained in F. S. Regs., Part II. and the Staff Manual respectively. Title pages will be prepared in manuscript.

WAR DIARY
or
INTELLIGENCE SUMMARY.
(Erase heading not required.)

Army Form C. 2118.

Place	Date	Hour	Summary of Events and Information	Remarks and references to Appendices
	29/7/15	-	Arrived at Havre in the early morning. Disembarked at 9 AM and entrained at 6 P.M.	
	30/7/15	4 P.M	Arrived at St OMER. Division billeted in G.H.Q. area. Divisional Hd Qrs at TILQUES.	
Tilques	31/7/15		At TILQUES. fixed up a place for my office. re-arranged some of the duties of Veterinary Officers of the Division to suit the grouping of the various units. Head Qrs allotted me the Austin Motor Car (15 H.P.) for my own use. Reported my arrival to D.V.S. H.Q. I.G.C.	
			W. A. Pallin Vety Major A.D.V.S. 37th Division	

1577 Wt. W10791/1773 500,000 1/15 D. D. & L. A.D.S.S./Forms/C. 2118.

WAR DIARY
or
INTELLIGENCE SUMMARY.
(Erase heading not required.)

Army Form C. 2118.

Instructions regarding War Diaries and Intelligence Summaries are contained in F. S. Regs., Part II. and the Staff Manual respectively. Title pages will be prepared in manuscript.

Place	Date	Hour	Summary of Events and Information	Remarks and references to Appendices
TILQUES	1/8/15		Morning. Office. Afternoon to 110th Infantry Brigade. 123rd + 124th Bde R.A. and saw Captain Jones and Lieut Waddell. the V.O.s of.	
"	2/8/15		Morning to see billets allotted to the 28th M.V.S. which is due to arrive tomorrow – To 125th & 126th Bde R.A. – and saw Lieut Stanford V.O. of the former unit. Afternoon to ANDUICQ and saw Lieut White there. attending to a horse which had been left there by the 126th Bde R.A. afterwards to 112th Infantry Bde and 291 Co A.S.C where I saw Lieut Heuston – and arranged to transfer him to the 124th Bde R.A tomorrow – now the 37th Divisional Train has been split up –	
"	3/8/15		28th Mobile Vety Section arrived at 10.30 A.M. and I visited them in the Billets and I handed the O.C. his letter. Orders to date. and a list showing the distribution of the Division – afterwards to Lostat and transferred Lieut Heustis from 291 Co A.S.C. to 124 Bde R A at POLINCOVE. Lieut Waddell from 124 Bde R.A to 123rd Bde R.A at RUMINGHEM. and Captain Jones from 123rd Bde RA to Yorkshire Dragoons at SERQUES – Returned to H.Qrs at 7 P.M to find orders in for a move in the morning. Had a notice put in Divisional Orders regarding animals unfit to march. and went round to see O.C Mobile Vety Section and gave him instructions regarding the march and collection of animals left behind –	

Instructions regarding War Diaries and Intelligence Summaries are contained in F. S. Regs., Part II. and the Staff Manual respectively. Title pages will be prepared in manuscript.

WAR DIARY
or
INTELLIGENCE SUMMARY.
(Erase heading not required.)

Army Form C. 2118.

Place	Date	Hour	Summary of Events and Information	Remarks and references to Appendices
Tilques.	4/8/15	9 AM	Visited the Mobile Vety Section. and took the O.C. round to see the D.H.Q. area re order of march for the Section – To St Omer & saw Captain Roche-Kelly V.O. at G.H.Q. regarding collection of any animals left behind in G.H.Q. area – Returned to Tilques. Packed up my office –	
			Afternoon visited M.V.S. again, and gave the final instructions re disposal of animals unfit to march – and then rode on to next billets inspecting the whole column right from the rear as I went. Noticed a very large number of shoes are being lost – and shoeing of Infantry. A.S.C. & R.E. is bad – and many of the mules have not been shod behind. Pointed these things out to the Transport officers along the road and also spoke to the Staff Captain 112 Inf Brigade in particular about their shoeing –	
			Arrived at RENESCURE at 5.30 p.m. and found a good billet for the M.V.S. 1 Kilo East of the village just between the HAZEBROUCK Road and the Railway.	
RENESCURE			Marched to CAESTRE via HAZEBROUCK where I met Col Wilson D.D.V.S. 2nd Army – and he arranged to come & see in the morning – Arrived at CAESTRE	

1577 Wt. W10791/1773 500,000 1/15 D. D. & L. A.D.S.S./Forms/C. 2118.

Instructions regarding War Diaries and Intelligence Summaries are contained in F. S. Regs., Part II. and the Staff Manual respectively. Title pages will be prepared in manuscript.

WAR DIARY
or
INTELLIGENCE SUMMARY.
(Erase heading not required.)

Army Form C. 2118.

Place	Date	Hour	Summary of Events and Information	Remarks and references to Appendices
CAESTRE	5/8/15		At Division reinforced area running N + S from St Sylvestre Cappel to HAZEBROUCK and W + E from HONEGHEM to FLETRE. Mobile Vety Section arrived at 6.30 pm and billeted in same field with Yorkshire Dragoons at CAESTRE as temporary measure – Spent evening fixing up my office –	
"	6/8/15		DDVS 2nd Army arrived at 10. AM and spent 1½ hours in my office going through various things and gave me a large file of memos & orders to copy out and circulate. Afternoon he inspected the N.C.O.'s & men of the Section & gave them an address. In the afternoon visited 28th Div A.H.Q. and went out in search of a suitable farm for the M.V.S. and found a nice one on the FLETRE. – STRAZEELE Road about 1 Kilo South of FLETRE. which I decided on. Good ~~[illegible]~~ accommodation for Officer N.C.O.s & men. an excellent field and ample water supply –	
"	7/8/15		M.V.S. moved into their new billets in the morning and I went out to see them at 12 noon and had a notice published in orders as to their location on my return – Officers to see 112 Inf Brigade – + 124 Bde R.A. HAZEBROUCK + HONEGHEM	
"	8/8/15		Found unit moved out to LOCRE to be attached to 28th Division to work out later there. Arranged to find Capt. Jones out there looking in Vety charge of ~~[illegible]~~ our troops in that area.	

Instructions regarding War Diaries and Intelligence Summaries are contained in F. S. Regs., Part II. and the Staff Manual respectively. Title pages will be prepared in manuscript.

WAR DIARY
or
INTELLIGENCE SUMMARY.
(Erase heading not required.)

Army Form C. 2118

Place	Date	Hour	Summary of Events and Information	Remarks and references to Appendices
CHESTRE	9/8/15	Morning.	D.D.V.S. 2nd Army called in for a few minutes. Afterwards I took Capt Jones out to LOCRE and left him out there – to M.V.S. on my return –	
"	10/8/15		Morning Office. to M.V.S. inspected all the cases and picked out those for discharge or evacuation. Afternoon to St Marie Cappel & Hazebrouck to see V.O. of R.A. & [illegible] who have now joined up, bringing another V.O. with them in temporary charge.	
"	11/8/15		Morning Office & to Cassel to see Gassing experiments – Afternoon – to [illegible] 288th A.S.C. & M.V.S. and had a circular memorandum published with orders about the Clipping – Got 1st week Army FORM off today in good time complete all except those the Office which A Office cannot produce –	
"	12/8/15		Office – visit to M.V.S.	
"	13/8/15		Office weekly Returns coming in all the morning. Afternoon, 1st Conference of V.O's – went through all the back circulars with them – and conference took nearly 3 hours – as there were many things to discuss especially method of sending animals to the M.V.S. and also the information about [illegible] left behind in billets –	
"	14/8/15 + 15/8/15		Office. Army FORM. A2000 despatched in good time –	
"	16/8/15		Morning Office – Afternoon to CROIX DE POPERINGE to see Capt JONES.	
"	17/8/15		Morning Office. & HAZEBROUCK. Afternoon to CROIX de POPERINGE & took Jones to NIEPPE and ARMENTIERE where we saw A.D.V.S. of the 12th & 50th Divisions	

1577 Wt. W10791/1773 500,000 1/15 D. D. & L. A.D.S.S./Forms/C. 2118.

Instructions regarding War Diaries and Intelligence Summaries are contained in F. S. Regs., Part II. and the Staff Manual respectively. Title pages will be prepared in manuscript.

WAR DIARY
or
INTELLIGENCE SUMMARY.
(Erase heading not required.)

Army Form C. 2118.

Place	Date	Hour	Summary of Events and Information	Remarks and references to Appendices
CAESTRE	18 8/15		Office – most of the day.	
"	19 8/15		Morning Office. Yorkshire Dragoons. 1st Div. Hd. Qrs. lines.	
			Afternoon. To LOCRE	
"	20 8/15		Morning. M.V.S. 28th Co A.S.C. & Remount Depot.	
			Afternoon. Office and Conference of V.O.s.	
"	21 8/15		Morning To R.A. Afternoon. Office	
"	22 8/15		Sunday. Army Form N 2000 completed & despatched.	
"	23 8/15		Morning to M.V.S. to inspect cases for evacuation. And on return to H.Q. heard that we were moving at once. Afternoon returned to M.V.S. & warned O.C. Section and ~~in~~ instructed him to clear the Hospital. Met D.D.V.S. at the Section looked round some cases he had sent in from the Remount Depot and he said that he would give any assistance he could for the move. To R.A. [illegible] and inspected some debilitated horses which they want to cast. and sent a number of them to the Section for evacuation –	
"	24 8/15		Morning to M.V.S. 28th Co A.S.C. & Yorkshire Dragoons. Afternoon to Nieppe, ~~and~~ collected Captain Jones kit and left him instructions to return to CAESTRE tonight and accompany the Yorkshire Dragoons tomorrow – Evening packed up office &c.	

1577 Wt. W10791/1773 500,000 1/15 D. D. & L. A.D.S.S./Forms/C. 2118.

Instructions regarding War Diaries and Intelligence Summaries are contained in F. S. Regs., Part II. and the Staff Manual respectively. Title pages will be prepared in manuscript.

WAR DIARY
or
INTELLIGENCE SUMMARY.
(Erase heading not required.)

Army Form C. 2118.

Place	Date	Hour	Summary of Events and Information	Remarks and references to Appendices
	25/2/15	9.30 am	Marched to GODEWAERVELDE with Head Qrts Transport &c and entrained for DOULLENS. Artillery entrained at CASSEL. We entrained at 11.15 am, left at 1.15 pm. Had intended to ~~[illegible]~~ visit the Section again before leaving and remain at CAESTRE for another to see most of the Division but being unable to get a car for either purpose had to go on with the H.Q. Transport.	
DOULLENS		8 p.m.	Arrived at DOULLENS – no arrangements made by the Staff for watering the horses in the train and as there was no one to conduct us to the Camping ground on arrival. There was very considerable delay before the animals were watered & fed & the men got settled in for the night. Camping ground which was a kind of dumping ground in the town was covered with much broken glass empty [illegible] and rubbish was most unsuitable –	
"	26/2/15		Fixed up my office in the Hotel de Ville in the same room as ~~[illegible]~~ D.A.D.O.S. & Camp Commandant & clerks –	
			Wire from D.D.V.S. 2nd Army that Lt ~~[illegible]~~ Prager V.C. 28 M.V.S. has been taken to Hospital and that he is sending Lieut Horsten on with the Section –	
			Morning visited Yorkshire Dragoons, saw Capt Town and instructed him to take over the Section as soon as it arrives. And we both went to have a look at the place allotted for the Section –	

1577 Wt. W10791/1773 500,000 1/15 D. D. & L. A.D.S.S./Forms/C. 2118.

Instructions regarding War Diaries and Intelligence Summaries are contained in F. S. Regs., Part II. and the Staff Manual respectively. Title pages will be prepared in manuscript.

WAR DIARY
or
INTELLIGENCE SUMMARY.
(Erase heading not required.)

Army Form C. 2118.

Place	Date	Hour	Summary of Events and Information	Remarks and references to Appendices
DOULLENS	26/8/15		(Continued) Afternoon. Went out to have another look at the place allotted for the Section and finally arranged with the Yorkshire Dragoons that they should give up one of the fields they were occupying to the Section.	
"	27/8/15		Morning. Office. Went to see Capt. Jones and make final arrangements about the reception of the Section. Afternoon to R.A. at THIEVRES and FAMECHON and rode to MONTECOURT to meet the Section which arrived there at 5 p.m. Gave Lt Huston his instructions saw the Section dismount and started on the road and advised Capt. Jones of their probable time of arrival so that he could have a look out man to meet them and show their billet and inform him of their arrival.	
"	28/8/15		Morning. Office - visited M.V.S. Captain Jones takes over command from Lt Huston and the latter returned to the 124 Bde R.A. Visited all the V.O's and gave them new Maps and showed them ~~to~~ the position of the Division - Brigades &c. Afternoon - visited 20th D.A.C & 9th North Staffords - collected some more Returns & spent evening in Office.	

1577 Wt. W10791/1773 500,000 1/15 D. D. & L. A.D.S.S./Forms/C. 2118.

Instructions regarding War Diaries and Intelligence Summaries are contained in F. S. Regs., Part II. and the Staff Manual respectively. Title pages will be prepared in manuscript.

Army Form C. 2118.

WAR DIARY
or
INTELLIGENCE SUMMARY.
(Erase heading not required.)

Place	Date	Hour	Summary of Events and Information	Remarks and references to Appendices
DOULLENS	29/8/15		Sunday Morning to M.V.S. for some information about Returns – Remainder of day taken up with Weekly Returns which I got finished and despatched in good time –	
	30/8/15		Morning To PAS with Chief Interpreter to see about billets for myself. my office and also for the Mobile Vety Section – Afternoon – Took Capt Jones out to GRINCOURT to prospect for a suitable FARM for the Section. There are several v good farms at present occupied by the 13th Regt of Field Artillery. but there is a great difficulty about water and all the animals would have to walk anything from a 1½ mile to ½ mile to water – also the farms are required for the 37th Divisional Train –	
	31/8/15		Morning. Office and to M.V.S. Afternoon to GRINCOURT with O.C. [illegible]. to inspect the farms [illegible] again – and practically decided not to try putting the Section so far forward –	
			W. A. Pallin. Vety Major. A.D.V.S. 37th Division.	

1577 Wt. W10791/1773 500,000 1/15 D. D. & L. A.D.S.S./Forms/C. 2118.

121/7153

37th Division

H.Q. 37th Division A.D.V.S.

Vol: 2

Sep/ 15

Instructions regarding War Diaries and Intelligence Summaries are contained in F. S. Regs., Part II. and the Staff Manual respectively. Title Pages will be prepared in manuscript.

WAR DIARY
or
INTELLIGENCE SUMMARY
(Erase heading not required.)

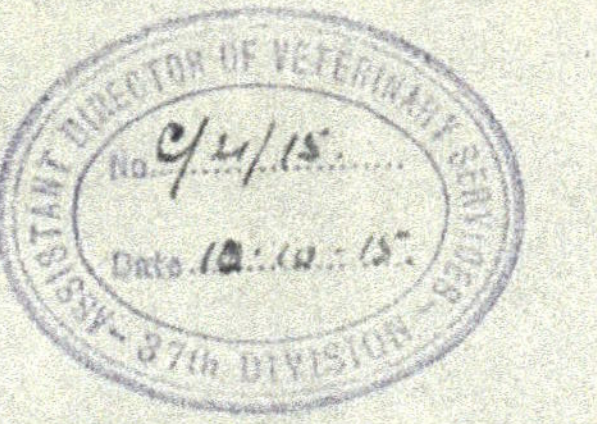

Army Form C. 2118

Place	Date	Hour	Summary of Events and Information	Remarks and references to Appendices
PAS.	29/9/15		Morning D.D.V.S. called and informed me that the HENU case had been diagnosed as Glanders – we went out there together. Met the C.R.A. of the Brigade. gave instructions to V.O. of Battery not [illegible] Mallein Testing of the A.C. 125 Bde. Afternoon to BUS to see A.D.V.S. 48th Division and consult him regarding the recent outbreak of Glanders in his Division – D.D.V.S. called in while I was there –	
"	30/9/15		Morning G.O.C. R.A. 7th Corps. came in to see me and consult me about the condition of the R.A. Horses – Afterwards I went to HENU to see that the V.O. of Bde made all his arrangements complete for starting the inoculations of the A.C. 125 Bde tonight – one subsection is to be done every second night – Afternoon – Had an interview with the C.R.A. on the condition of the R.A. Horses – Afterwards to MONDICOURT and on to GRENAS with V.O. of D.A.C. to see another mule which has died suddenly – P.M.E. revealed Ruptured Stomach – examination of the Blood negative – W. A. Pallin. Vety Major. A.D.V.S. 37th Division	

1875 Wt. W593/826 1,000,000 4/15 J.B.C. & A. A.D.S.S./Forms/C. 2118.

WAR DIARY
or
INTELLIGENCE SUMMARY
(Erase heading not required.)

Army Form C. 2118.

Instructions regarding War Diaries and Intelligence Summaries are contained in F. S. Regs., Part II. and the Staff Manual respectively. Title Pages will be prepared in manuscript.

Place	Date	Hour	Summary of Events and Information	Remarks and references to Appendices
PAS.	26 9/15		Sunday – Finished A 2000 and Anthrax Report in the morning – Afternoon to HENU to see some cases – and saw 2 very suspicious cases of Glanders in AC/121 Bde. – Took all the necessary precautions – and arranged to test them and the contacts tomorrow night –	
"	27 9/15		Morning to HENU inspected the suspicious and contact cases again – and made arrangements to Test them with Mallein tonight – afterwards to La COUCHIE, LE BESQUE FARM, GAUDIEMPRE, WARLINCOURT and MONDICOURT where all my V.O.s warned about the suspicious cases and at the Mobile Vety Section inspected 3 horses from the suspected unit – gave instructions for them to be tested and for information re any evacuated animals from that unit to be sent at once to the Base. Warned all V.O.s to attend at HENU in the morning. Reported the case to H.Q. Division. H.Q. Div R.A. informed and by wire to the D.D.V.S. 3rd Army.	
"	28 9/15		Morning Office – 10 AM to HENU – meeting of all V.O.s + DDVS at 10.30 AM to view the cases – none of them have Re-action – and any suspicion of Glanders are practically cleared up. but DDVS thinks Mallein may be stale or that the fact that the Temperatures not being normal at time of inoculation – or the condition of the case may account for the Non-Reaction. The two 121 cases were destroyed and examined. All Glanders precautions being taken. P.M.s were interesting but lesions found were not typical of Glanders – DDVS took specimens to Abbeville for	microscopical examination –

1875 Wt. W593/826 1,000,000 4/15 J.B.C. & A. A.D.S.S./Forms/C. 2118.

Instructions regarding War Diaries and Intelligence Summaries are contained in F. S. Regs., Part II. and the Staff Manual respectively. Title Pages will be prepared in manuscript.

WAR DIARY
or
INTELLIGENCE SUMMARY
(Erase heading not required.)

Army Form C. 2118.

Place	Date	Hour	Summary of Events and Information	Remarks and references to Appendices
PAS	22.9.15		Morning To HENU to see that the Disinfection &c was being carried out satisfactorily afterwards to GAUDIEMPRE and back via WARLINCOURT to see O.C. 37th Div. Train + make arrangements about Capt Jones going there - Afternoon to MONDICOURT to see Lt Payne who is taking over the Section from Capt Jones today - then on to GRENAS to see about another death in the D.A.C. which died suddenly last night - carcase has all the appearance of Anthrax. so simply had hind limb taken and case dealt with as Anthrax -	
			Captain Jones transferred to WARLINCOURT and took over 37th Div. Train from Lt White -	
			Sent wire to D.D.V.S reporting another case of Anthrax in D.A.C at GRENAS.	
"	23.9.15		No definite report from Laboratory about the HENU case, but so far all the evidence goes to show that they were Anthrax and not poisoning - so they are being returned as such.	
			Morning D.D.V.S. 3rd Army came over and I went with him out to HENU to see how things were getting on and to see that the Disinfection &c was being satisfactorily carried out -	
			Afternoon - I went to Mondicourt to M.V.S. and on to GRENAS and back by the Yorkshire Dragoons -	
"	24.9.15		Morning & afternoon Office - Conference of V.O's. and discussed all about the HENU cases. Anthrax &c.	
"	25.9.15		Morning Office. D.D.V.S called - and I went with him to MONDICOURT and he inspected the M.V.S.	
			Afternoon. Office. and wrote report on HENU + GRENAS cases of Anthrax -	

Instructions regarding War Diaries and Intelligence Summaries are contained in F. S. Regs., Part II. and the Staff Manual respectively. Title Pages will be prepared in manuscript.

WAR DIARY
or
INTELLIGENCE SUMMARY
(Erase heading not required.)

Army Form C. 2118.

Place	Date	Hour	Summary of Events and Information	Remarks and references to Appendices
PAS	18/9/16		Morning reported the case by wire to D.D.V.S. 3rd Army. To MUNDICOURT and GRENAS to see D.A.C. and see that all antiseptic precautions had been taken – ~~Afternoon~~ Afternoon to 125th & 124 Bde R.A. to see the V.O. i/c and interview the A.V.C. who have arrived –	
"	19/9/16		Sunday – Morning & afternoon – Office –	
"	20/9/16		Morning. Report from Lt Stanford that one horse had died suddenly at HENU in C/125 Bde on Saturday night and another this morning – I told him to go & take all antiseptic precautions and later I went out to see them & put in writing orders myself. Isolated ~~at~~ burial ground, etc. afterwards to interview the A.V.C. Sergeants there & others in the Inf Brigades & GAUDIEMPRE to see the Veterinaries – and on return in the evening found that there was a report in from HENU that 3 more horses had died in D/126 shortly after return from water – & that poisoning was now suspected. Went out there at once – & made all inquiries but as it was now dark – one could not do much until the morning. except have contacts isolated and all antiseptic precautions taken – wired reporting the 3 fresh deaths to D.A.V.S. on my return –	
"	21/9/16		Morning to HENU – & began making arrangements to bring the 3 carcases to make P.M.E. in the grave. D.A.V.S. arrived shortly afterwards & superintended the Post Mortems – which took some time. In the afternoon I took the specimens to BEAVAL for examination. Lieut Pryor returned from sick leave & took over the station –	

1875 Wt. W593/826 1,000,000 4/15 J.B.C. & A. A.D.S.S./Forms/C. 2118.

Instructions regarding War Diaries and Intelligence Summaries are contained in F. S. Regs., Part II. and the Staff Manual respectively. Title Pages will be prepared in manuscript.

WAR DIARY
or
INTELLIGENCE SUMMARY
(Erase heading not required.)

Army Form C. 2118

Place	Date	Hour	Summary of Events and Information	Remarks and references to Appendices
PAS	14/9/15		Morning to 37th Div Train to see how my orders re Anthrax precautions were being carried out. Made further enquiries in the District from the Maire in GRINCOURT and also from M AVCHARD at PAS but could get no information as to any previous outbreaks in this District. Afternoon – to BIENVILLERS to 111th Inf Bde H.Q. – Afternoon completed Report on ANTHRAX and gave it to clerk to type.	
"	15/9/15		Morning – Office sent off Anthrax report. Visited M.V.S. went through three cases for evacuation and several other matters. – Afternoon took OC M.V.S. with DOULLENS to see R.T.O. R.S.O. and arrange about despatch of animals to the Base. Also made arrangements with a Frenchman who owns some land near the Station, to stand the horses in his field while awaiting Trucks & loading if necessary, water there – also a barn there for the night. – Returned via SARTON and visited the 48th M.V.S. & called in to see Yorkshire Dragoons on the way back. D.D.V.S. called while I was out.	
"	16/9/15		Morning. Office. To Yorkshire Dragoons – ~~afternoon to~~ afternoon to 6th North Staffords & 37th Div Train – and on return found that Capt Towne had been to report another previous case of Anthrax in the D.A.C. which died last night.	
"	17/9/15		Morning – Office. Nothing wrt A.2000 for H.Q. mob. D.D.V.S. called & went through list of A.V.C. Sergeants. Afternoon. Office & conference of V.O.'s. – Discussed the subject of Anthrax & other topics. Later took ~~anthrax~~ specimen to Mobile Laboratory at BEAVAL for microscopical examination leaving a note with it. Later got a wire saying it was Anthrax.	

Instructions regarding War Diaries and Intelligence Summaries are contained in F. S. Regs., Part II. and the Staff Manual respectively. Title pages will be prepared in manuscript.

WAR DIARY
or
INTELLIGENCE SUMMARY.
(Erase heading not required.)

Army Form C. 2118.

Place	Date	Hour	Summary of Events and Information	Remarks and references to Appendices
PAS.	10/9/15		Morning Office – To HENU to the Remount which I tried to find last evening – also interviewed Farrier Sergt LUNT D/126 with a view to his transfer to the A.V.C. – Afternoon Office & conference of	V.O.'s
"	11/9/15		Morning Office and Yorkshire Dragoons. Afternoon to WARLINCOURT ~~[illegible]~~ to investigate a case in	37th Train
			which is reported by the V.O. i/c to have died from colic and on P.M.E. showed symptoms of ANTHRAX	
"	12/9/15		Sunday – Morning & afternoon Office – Report at 8pm from Abbeville saying [illegible] from horse in No 1 Coy 37th Div. Train is Anthrax – Reported the case by wire to D.D.V.S. 3rd Army and made verbal report to DA & QMG & AA & QMG and also went out and reported the matter to OC Train personally – pointed out to him again the seriousness of the case and impressed upon him the necessity of taking and carrying out the strictest precautions –	
"	13/9/15		Morning – to GAUDIEMPRE to see Lt White and inform re diagnosis of the case of Anthrax in his charge at WARLINCOURT, urged upon him the necessity of seeing that all the necessary precautions were carried out. Afterwards to St AMAND to see VO 126 Bde re the same Remount. Struck by the 37th Div. Train to see that they were complying with the ANTHRAX precautions – 1.45pm A.D.V.S. 3rd Army arrived and I accompanied him to GAUDIEMPRE to see what was being done about the Anthrax – and he gave some further instructions and pointed out to Lt White the necessity of seeing the work done himself [illegible] in the subject of the cause. Evening office writing reports.	

WAR DIARY
or
INTELLIGENCE SUMMARY.
(Erase heading not required.)

Army Form C. 2118.

Instructions regarding War Diaries and Intelligence Summaries are contained in F. S. Regs., Part II. and the Staff Manual respectively. Title pages will be prepared in manuscript.

Place	Date	Hour	Summary of Events and Information	Remarks and references to Appendices
DOULLENS	4/9/15		Morning to M.V.S. and 288 Coy A.S.C. about weekly returns – and afternoon to Mailly Mailly + LIELVILLER to see 112th ~~Bde~~ Infantry Bde + 291 Co A.S.C. who are attached to the 4th Division for instruction – Evening got A. 2000 finished. all correspondence up to date. and packed up office ready to move –	
"	5/9/15		Move to PAS. and take up our position in the line.	
PAS	6/9/15		Morning Office – Re-arranging duties owing to alteration in re-distribution of the Troops. Afternoon to St Amand, where I met Lt Heaton on his rounds – and I left a note for Lt White to move to QUADIEMPRE – afterwards on to SOUASTRE and Mechanical Transport to HENU and finally on to MONDICOURT to see the Mobile Vety Section. who have arrived there and find their billet very comfortable. but they have lots of work to do to get the place cleaned up – and put in order –	
"	7/9/15		Morning to GAUDIEMPRE – afternoon to M.V.S	
"	8/9/15		Morning Office. and to visit 37th Div Train. Afternoon to POMMIER to see 110th Inf Brigade.	
"	9/9/15		Morning. D.D.V.S. arranged to come and inspect the M.V.S. but he cancelled his arrangements and did not come. Visited ~~GA~~ GAUDIEMPRE. LA BEZQUE FARM (to see Field Surgeon re transfer to A.V.C.) and afterwards on to LA COUCHIE. – Afternoon to AUTHIE and home by HENU where I went to see a Remount in C/126 which is reported to have arrived lame –	

1577 Wt. W10791/1773 500,000 1/15 D. D. & L. A.D.S.S./Forms/C. 2118.

Instructions regarding War Diaries and Intelligence Summaries are contained in F. S. Regs., Part II. and the Staff Manual respectively. Title pages will be prepared in manuscript.

WAR DIARY

or

INTELLIGENCE SUMMARY.

(Erase heading not required.)

Army Form C. 2118.

Place	Date	Hour	Summary of Events and Information	Remarks and references to Appendices
DOULLENS	1/9/15		Morning Office. and to CANDAS to see D.A.C. While I was out Lt Col Ake D.D.V.S. 3rd Army called to see me. also Lt Col Harris A.D.V.S. 4th Division called later and I had a consultation with him on matters of interest.	
			Afternoon. Office and informed the Head Qrs Staff that I should like to have the Mobile Vety. Section to be at Mondicourt when we move into ~~our~~ our new area. This was arranged. and I was given permission to go to Mondicourt and look for a suitable site to billet the Section.	
"	2/9/15		Morning. Office and to Mobile Vety Section.	
			Afternoon to Mondicourt accompanied by the Section Interpreter to see about billets and settled to take the Old Chocolate Factory - where there is excellent accomodation for the Officers. N.C.Os. men - also some good stabling existing and other accomodation which can easily be improved upon. good water laid on - and Electric light. and also splendid orchard for Pick Lines as long as we wish to keep the animals in the open.	
"	3/9/15		Morning. Inspected all the H.Q. animals and made out A2000. for H.Q. also to visit D.A.C at CANDAS and compile their return.	
			Afternoon - Office -	

1577 Wt. W10791/1773 500,000 1/15 D. D. & L. A.D.S.S./Forms/C. 2118.

121/7595

H.Q. 37th Div: A.D.M.S.

Vol 3

Oct 15

nil

Cm

Instructions regarding War Diaries and Intelligence Summaries are contained in F. S. Regs., Part II. and the Staff Manual respectively. Title pages will be prepared in manuscript.

WAR DIARY
or
INTELLIGENCE SUMMARY.
(Erase heading not required.)

Army Form C. 2118.

Place	Date	Hour	Summary of Events and Information	Remarks and references to Appendices
PAS.	26/10/15		Morning Inspected 19th Heavy Battery, & 3 Companies of R.E.	
			Afternoon. Office.	
"	27/10/15		Morning. Inspected H.Q. Company 37th Div Train.	
			Afternoon. – 49th Field Ambulance.	
"	28/10/15		Morning Office. Afternoon. Inspected Supply Section of the 37th Div Train.	
"	29/10/15		Morning. Inspected D.H.Q. Horses &c. Office.	
			Afternoon – Conference of V.O.'s & Office.	
"	30/10/15		Morning – Inspected No. 3 Company. 37th Divisional Train.	
			Afternoon – Office.	
"	31/10/15		Sunday – Morning Inspected Companies Nos 2 & 4. 37th Divisional Train.	
			Afternoon – Office.	

W. A. Pallin. Vety Major
A.D.V.S. 37th Division

T2134. Wt. W708–776. 500000. 4/15. Sir J. C. & S.

WAR DIARY
or
INTELLIGENCE SUMMARY.
(Erase heading not required.)

Army Form C. 2118.

Instructions regarding War Diaries and Intelligence Summaries are contained in F. S. Regs., Part II. and the Staff Manual respectively. Title pages will be prepared in manuscript.

Place	Date	Hour	Summary of Events and Information	Remarks and references to Appendices
PAS	20/10/15		(Continued) Post Mortem Examinations were carried out but as there were complications of Suppurated Strangles and Pyaemia the lesions present were not to my mind typical.	
			Afternoon with Major Holiday to Bienvillers - and back via HENU to see AC of 125 Bde again.	
"	21/10/15		Morning to MONDICOURT for Major Holiday, who came with me to HENU and had a final look at the horses of the AC/125 Bde - afterwards back to my office - then he went through some circulars with me and I gave him copies of my own circulars - Afternoon took Major Holiday to GRINCOURT to see the Water Trough we had built there and back via GAUDIEMPRE and HENU.	
"	22/10/15		Morning received Major Holiday's report and forwarded it to D.D.V.S. with my remarks attached.	
			Took Major Holiday with me out to POMMIER to inspect 110th Inf Brigade - 1/1/2 Co R.E. also on the way I inspected some Remount mules issued to the 124th Bde R.F.A. - Afternoon conference of V.O's. - Major Holiday present.	
"	23/10/15		Morning - Took Major Holiday to La COUCHIE to see a suspected case of Anthrax in D/Battery 123rd Bde RFA.	
			Afternoon Major Holiday left for Abbeville -	
"	24/10/15		Sunday - Got A.F. A2000 weekly reports all finished - and all correspondence up to date, and had a visit from the A.D.V.S., 48th Division -	
"	25/10/15		Morning - Inspected 37th D.A.C. animals for casting, also went through cases for evacuation at the M.H.	
			Afternoon. Office -	

T2134. Wt. W708—776. 500000. 4/15. Sir J. C. & S.

Instructions regarding War Diaries and Intelligence Summaries are contained in F. S. Regs., Part II. and the Staff Manual respectively. Title Pages will be prepared in manuscript.

WAR DIARY
or
INTELLIGENCE SUMMARY
(Erase heading not required.)

Army Form C. 2118

Place	Date	Hour	Summary of Events and Information	Remarks and references to Appendices
PAS	17/10/15		Sunday. Morning visit from D.D.V.S. and went with him to HENU to see animals HQ/125 Bde which are still under suspicion for Glanders. after which he visited our Head Qrts and had an interview with the A.A & Q.M.G.	
			Afternoon. Office. Finished weekly Reports and got all correspondence up to date.	
"	18/10/15		Morning visited M.V.S. and went through cases for evacuation.	
			Afternoon - visited HENU and made final arrangements for the inoculation of the HQ/125 Bde which is to be carried out by Major Hobday in the morning.	
"		5 pm	D.D.V.S. arrived with Major Hobday at my Office when I took him to Mondicourt and put him up with the O.C. M.V.S. as I had no accomodation for him here.	
"	19/10/15		Morning. to HENU with Major Hobday. who carried out the Intra-Palpebral Mallein Inoculation all my V.O.s being present except Lt Pryor. who had a special demonstration at the M.V.S. also present where the D.D.V.S. 3rd Army. and the A.D.V.S. of the 36th & 48th Divisions.	
			Afternoon — Took Major Hobday with me to see the 37th Divisional Train.	
"	20/10/15		Morning to HENU with Major Hobday. all V.O.s attended as also did the A.D.V.S. of the 36th & 48th Division & D.D.V.S. 3rd Army. 4 Horses already under suspicion have re-acted to the Test and were destroyed as Glanders.	

1875 Wt. W593/826 1,000,000 4/15 J.B.C. & A. A.D.S.S./Forms/C. 2118.

Instructions regarding War Diaries and Intelligence Summaries are contained in F. S. Regs., Part II. and the Staff Manual respectively. Title Pages will be prepared in manuscript.

WAR DIARY
or
INTELLIGENCE SUMMARY
(Erase heading not required.)

Army Form C. 2118

Place	Date	Hour	Summary of Events and Information	Remarks and references to Appendices
PAS	10/10/15		Sunday – Morning to 124th Bde and inspected their Debility cases and picked out 10 horses for immediate evacuation. Afternoon. Office –	
"	11/10/15		D.D.R. is unable to spare any more time to accompany me at my inspections. So have to finish the inspection by myself. Morning. Inspected 125th Bde. Afternoon to M.V.S. and inspected cases for evacuation –	
"	12/10/15		Morning. Inspected 37th Divisional Ammunition Column –	
"	13/10/15		Morning. Attended inspection of 111th & 112th Inf Bde 1st Line Transport – by Brig-Gen. Fox R.A. from Corps HQ – with G.S.O. 1 + A A + Q M G of the Division. a very fine lot of horses and animals all in very good condition – Afternoon. Office and to M.V.S.	
"	14/10/15		Morning to HENU and inspected the Debility cases of the 125 + 126 Bde – picked out a certain number for evacuation. Afternoon to BIENVILLERS to HENU and on to FAMECHON.	
"	15/10/15		Morning attend inspection by G.O.C. Division of the Yorkshire Dragoons – Afternoon – Conference of V.O.s	
"	16/10/15		Morning. Visit from D.D.V.S. and went with him to HENU to see isolated animals of 125 Bde. Afternoon – Office. Wrote Weekly Return [struck out] finished all except Summary –	

1875 Wt. W593/826 1,000,000 4/15 J.B.C. & A. A.D.S.S./Forms/C. 2118.

Instructions regarding War Diaries and Intelligence Summaries are contained in F. S. Regs., Part II. and the Staff Manual respectively. Title Pages will be prepared in manuscript.

WAR DIARY
or
INTELLIGENCE SUMMARY
(Erase heading not required.)

Army Form C. 2118

Place	Date	Hour	Summary of Events and Information	Remarks and references to Appendices
PAS	4.10.15		(Continued) so altogether there will be very comfortable.	
"	5.10.15		Morning. D.D.R & self inspected the 123rd Bde R.F.A. Afternoon – To HENU to see how Mallein Testing and suspicious cases were progressing.	
"	6.10.15		Office most of the day.	
"	7.10.15		Morning D.D.R. and self inspected 126th Bde. A & B Battery & B.A.C. at HENU. also 20th Heavy Battery & 141st C.R.E. at the same & H.Q. 126th Bde at St. AMAND. Afternoon Inspected C & D. Battery 126 Bde at SOUASTRE. Evening Office.	
"	8.10.15		Morning. Visit from D.D.V.S. and I went with him to HENU to see the Doubtful Re-actors & other suspicious cases belonging to ~~the~~ the A.C./125 Bde. Afternoon – Conference of V.O's. Evening received report that another Mule had died suddenly at GRENAS	
"	9.10.15		Morning to GRENAS to see the Mule which died suddenly last evening – as it appears the another case of Anthrax. took all precautions & made no Post Mortem. Later on to 123rd Bde and picked out a number of Debilitated horses for evacuation. 15 Horses sent to M.V.S at once. Afternoon. Office – completed weekly Returns & Reports.	

1875 Wt. W593/826 1,000,000 4/15 J.B.C. & A. A.D.S.S./Forms/C. 2118.

Instructions regarding War Diaries and Intelligence Summaries are contained in F. S. Regs., Part II. and the Staff Manual respectively. Title Pages will be prepared in manuscript.

Army Form C. 2118

WAR DIARY
or
INTELLIGENCE SUMMARY
(Erase heading not required.)

Place	Date	Hour	Summary of Events and Information	Remarks and references to Appendices
PAS.	1 10/15.		Morning to COUIN to see Major Hobday carry out the intra-dermal Palpebral Mallein inoculation on the horses of a Battery belonging to the 48th Division – in the presence of the D.D.V.S. ~~and~~ most of the A.D.V.S. of the 3rd Army – plus the V.O.s of the 48th Division –	
			~~Afternoon~~ Afternoon to HENU to see results of mallein inoculation on C Subsection A/125 Bde. Only one animal shows any sign of Re-acting & he had fever at the time of inoculation and really looks more like a case of suppressed strangles – no animals reacted so look very little.	
"	2 10/15.		Morning to COUIN to see the result of the Mallein Testings – afternoon with D.D.V.S. to HENU to see results of new inoculations, and inspect suspicious cases –	
			Afternoon – Office – wrote Report on the case of Glanders at HENU	
"	3 10/15		Sunday – Morning to HENU to see Mallein Testings – Afternoon – Office and got A.F. A 2000 and Glanders Report finished –	
"	4 10/15		Morning – Began a joint Inspection of the animals of the Division with the D.D. Remounts 3rd Army – Inspected 124 Bde R.F.A. and noted a number of animals for evacuation.	
			Afternoon – To M.V.S. and inspected cases for evacuation to the Base – also inspected their arrangements for winter quarters. O.C. 28 M.V.S. has already got his (2) good shed built and 2 more in process of building – also he has made excellent standings with cinders and is able to obtain saw dust for Bedding – He has got a new Pharmacy and made arrangements to give the men improved dressing rooms…	

Wt. W593/826 1,000,000 4/15 J.B.C. & A. A.D.S.S./Forms/C. 2118.

HQ. 37th Div:
ADMS.
Vol: 4

121/7693

Nov. 15

Instructions regarding War Diaries and Intelligence Summaries are contained in F. S. Regs., Part II. and the Staff Manual respectively. Title pages will be prepared in manuscript.

WAR DIARY
or
INTELLIGENCE SUMMARY.
(*Erase heading not required.*)

Army Form C. 2118.

Place	Date	Hour	Summary of Events and Information	Remarks and references to Appendices
PAS.	25 11/15		Morning - Visited & Inspected Horses of 123 Bde R.F.A. - 37th Divisional Train & 9th Batt North Staffords - Afternoon Office.	JLCJ
	26 11/15		Morning - Visited & Inspected Horses of ~~[illegible]~~ 16th Bde - R.G.A. 37th Div Train & the 9th North Staffords - Afternoon Office interviewed V.O.s of Units.	JLCJ
	27 11/15		Morning. Visited 9th North Staffords - 37th Div Train Afternoon Office Visited Horses at Divisional Head Quarters	JLCJ
	28 11/15		Morning Visited Horses of Divisional Train & 9th North Staffords Attended Office.	JLCJ
	29 11/15		Morning Visited & Inspected Horses 25th M.V.S. Afternoon Office.	JLCJ
	30 11/15		Morning. Visited Yorkshire Dragoons & Sick & Lame Horses, also 37th Div Train Afternoon Office	JLCJ
	1. 12/15		Morning - Office & Attended Sick Lame Horses 37th Div Train Afternoon Office	JLCJ

W. Patton. Major
A.D.V.S. 37th Division

T2134. Wt. W708–776. 500000. 4/15. Sir J. C. & S.

Instructions regarding War Diaries and Intelligence Summaries are contained in F. S. Regs., Part II. and the Staff Manual respectively. Title pages will be prepared in manuscript.

WAR DIARY
or
INTELLIGENCE SUMMARY.
(Erase heading not required.)

Army Form C. 2118.

Place	Date	Hour	Summary of Events and Information	Remarks and references to Appendices
PAS	20/11/15		Morning Office and visited M.V.S. – Afternoon. To St AMAND and inspected the 10th Batt Loyal North Lan Regt. who have had cases of Sarcoptic Mange.	
			Evening Office – A.F. A2000 monthly report completed.	W.A.P.
"	21/11/15		Morning – Sunday – Office – and visited HENU with DAA & QMG to see Horse Standings of 125th & 126th Bde RFA – Some of them are getting on fairly well but all are still backward – Captain Jones came to lunch and afterwards went through some office work. Visited the M.V.S. with him, where we went through the cases for evacuation – Evening Office and got everything up to date prior to going on leave.	W.A.P.
"	22/11/15		Left on 8 days leave for ENGLAND – Captain J.L.C. JONES takes over the duties of A.D.V.S. during my absence.	W.A.P.
			Took over temporary duty as A.D.V.S. from Major W.A. Pallin. Visited 37th Divisional Train & 9th North Staffords. Afternoon Attended Office, also Visited & Examined Horses Divisional Head Quarters	J.L.C.J.
	23/11/15		Morning – Examined Horses "Sick & Lame" 37th Div Train – Afternoon Office & Visited Squadron Yorks Dragoons	J.L.C.J.
	24/11/15		Morning – Examined Horses 37th Div Train & 9th N. Staffords. Afternoon Office & Visited Horses Div Head Quarters	J.L.C.J.

T2134. Wt. W708–776. 500000. 4/15. Sir J. C. & S.

Instructions regarding War Diaries and Intelligence Summaries are contained in F. S. Regs., Part II. and the Staff Manual respectively. Title pages will be prepared in manuscript.

WAR DIARY
or
INTELLIGENCE SUMMARY.
(Erase heading not required.)

Army Form C. 2118.

Place	Date	Hour	Summary of Events and Information	Remarks and references to Appendices
PAS	14/11/15		Sunday – Morning Office – Afternoon – Wrote letters –	[initials]
"	15/11/15		Morning. Interview with G.O.C. on the subject of the number of admissions in the 125 Bde R.F.A. and discussed the question of standings, hard [illegible] & shelter – and invited him to come and inspect the Mobile Vety Section at an early date – Afternoon to M.V.S. and inspected the cases for evacuation – Afternoon. To GANDIEMPRE to make inquiries re Farriers & Shoeing Smiths in the 16th Bde R.G.A. – Evening Office –	[initials]
"	16/11/15		Heavy fall of snow in the early morning. – Office all day – but standings are very bad	[initials]
"	17/11/15		Morning. Inspected the 16th Bde R.G.A. – Horses are in very good condition, but they have a large number of wound Contused Treads & too much feathering etc. Several cases require to be sent to the M.V.S. at once. – Afternoon. Office –	[initials]
"	18/11/15		Morning – To GANDIEMPRE with D.A.A. & Q.M.G. to select new sites for standings for the 16th Bde R.G.A. & other pieces of their billeting which require some re-distribution – Afternoon to GRENAS to see a mule that died suddenly – Evening Office –	[initials]
"	19/11/15		Morning – Inspected D.H.Q. & 49th Field Ambulance. Afternoon. Office & Conference of V.O.s	[initials]

T2134. Wt. W708–776. 500000. 4/15. Sir J. C. & S.

Instructions regarding War Diaries and Intelligence Summaries are contained in F. S. Regs., Part II. and the Staff Manual respectively. Title pages will be prepared in manuscript.

WAR DIARY
or
INTELLIGENCE SUMMARY.
(Erase heading not required.)

Army Form C. 2118.

Place	Date	Hour	Summary of Events and Information	Remarks and references to Appendices
PAS	7.11.15		Sunday – Morning Office – Afternoon Inspected 9th North Stafford Regt (Pioneers)	WMT
"	8.11.15		Morning Office – To La COUCHIE to see OC 16th Bde. R.G.A. re Lt Richardson duties – and arranged to inspect the Brigade on the 17th inst.	WMT
			Afternoon. A.D.V.S. 48th Division called to inquire about a lost horse – after which I went to M.V.S. and inspected cases for evacuation –	
"	9.11.15		Morning. Office and visited the M.V.S.	WMT
			Afternoon. Lt Richardson V.O. of 16th R.G.A. Bde called in and I went through the memoranda with him.	
"	10.11.15		Morning – To AMIENS to purchase some microscopical apparatus – Gazettes sent to A.V.C. for R.H.Q.	WMT
			Evening. Office. Received report from Jones that he had returned from the 37th Division	
"	11.11.15		Morning Office – To GRENAS to inspect new Batch of H.D. Horses which have come to replace a draft of mules transferred to another Division – They are rather poor condition and the clipping is very bad. Afternoon – Office.	WMT
"	12.11.15		Morning Office – Inspected D.H.Q. & 49th Field Ambulance.	WMT
			Afternoon – Office and Conference of V.O.s	
"	13.11.15		Morning. Office & the 37th Div. Train –	WMT
			Afternoon. Office – A.F. A2000 fortnightly report completed –	

T2134. Wt. W708–776. 500000. 4/15. Sir J. C. & S.

Army Form C. 2118

Instructions regarding War Diaries and Intelligence Summaries are contained in F. S. Regs., Part II. and the Staff Manual respectively. Title pages will be prepared in manuscript.

WAR DIARY
or
INTELLIGENCE SUMMARY.
(Erase heading not required.)

Place	Date	Hour	Summary of Events and Information	Remarks and references to Appendices
PAS	1/11/15		Morning - To HENU to see Lieut Stanford about some friction which has arisen between him and the T.C. Wagon Lines C/126 Bde about moving some sick horses - at the same I inspected the 50 Field Ambulance horse lines - they have an excellent large hay shed for their animals quite the best in this area -	WNT
			Afternoon - To M.V.S. and inspected the animals for evacuation -	
"	2/11/15		Morning & Afternoon - Office.	WNT
"	3/11/15		Morning - To FAMECHON and inspected the Yorkshire Dragoons camp for casting - also saw their arrangements for the winter - they clipped a good many of their horses - leaving saddle patch & their legs - and they are all under cover.	WNT
			Afternoon. Office.	
"	4/11/15		Morning - To HENU to see Lieut Stanford and find him in bed with a bad cold. afterwards on to the 111th Inf Brigade HQrs. Afternoon - Office -	WNT
"	5/11/15		Morning Office and inspected Hd Qrs animals - Afternoon - Office & conference of V.O.'s.	WNT
"	6/11/15		Morning Office and to HENU to see Lt Stanford whom I found in bed with a bad cold and to (Captain Jones left for BOUVELLES to assist 27th Division with Mallein Testing.) GAUDIEMPRE and met Lieut Richardson A.V.C. who has arrived there i/c 16th Bde R.G.A. from 56th Division	WNT

T2134. Wt. W708–776. 500000. 4/15. Sir J. C. & S.

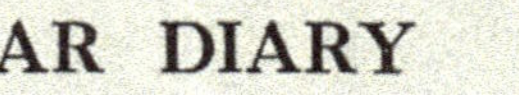

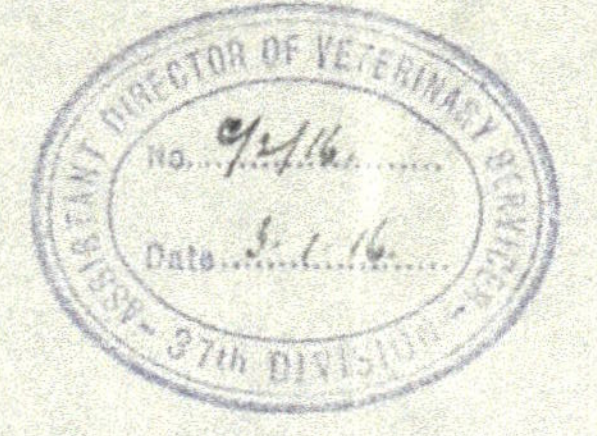

Army Form C. 2118

Instructions regarding War Diaries and Intelligence Summaries are contained in F. S. Regs., Part II. and the Staff Manual respectively. Title Pages will be prepared in manuscript.

WAR DIARY
or
INTELLIGENCE SUMMARY
(Erase heading not required.)

Place	Date	Hour	Summary of Events and Information	Remarks and references to Appendices
PAS	21 12/15		Morning. Office – Afternoon to HENU to see [illegible] – and visited one horse in the evening again.	[illegible]
"	22 12/15		Morning to HENU & office. Afternoon – to M.V.S. to investigate a charge against an N.C.O. Lieut Pryce placed on the Sick List & Captain Jones placed in temporary charge	[illegible]
"	23 12/15		Morning to HENU & carried out P.M.E. on Horse No 101 A/123 Bde which succumbed to the Test. D.D.V.S attended. Visited Lieut Pryce in the Field Ambulance. Afterwards went out to GAUDIEMPRE – Afternoon ~~to 37 Div Train & [illegible]~~ Office.	[illegible]
"	24 12/15		Morning to GAUDIEMPRE – Afternoon to 37th Div Train – [illegible] re [illegible] 37 Reserve Park & A/123 Bde	[illegible]
"	25 12/15		Xmas Day – Morning to see Lieut Pryce who is in Hospital – Afternoon – Office.	[illegible]
"	26 12/15		Sunday – Morning Office. To GAUDIEMPRE to make a P.M.E. on Horse No 118. 9th Heavy Battery RGA which reacted to Mallein – A.D.V.S attended – Afternoon – Office & finished weekly Report.	Lieut Pryce evacuated to Clearing Station
"	27 12/15		Office. Visited [illegible] Dragoons M.V.S. [illegible] animals for evacuation – Afternoon Office.	[illegible]
"	28 12/15		Office all day.	[illegible]
"	29 12/15		Morning Office visited Div. Train – Afternoon – Office	[illegible]
"	30 12/15		Morning to [illegible] inspected A/123 Bde & B/123 Bde for Mange. Afternoon – Office.	[illegible]
"	31 12/15		Morning Office and to ~~[illegible]~~ GAUDIEMPRE to inspect B/126 Bde & found that they have [illegible] case of [illegible] which the V.O. has not reported – Afternoon Office [illegible] Mange [illegible] Captain R.A. re [illegible]	[illegible]

1-1-1916 [illegible] Major A.D.V.S. 37th Division

Instructions regarding War Diaries and Intelligence Summaries are contained in F. S. Regs., Part II. and the Staff Manual respectively. Title pages will be prepared in manuscript.

WAR DIARY
or
INTELLIGENCE SUMMARY.
(Erase heading not required.)

Army Form C. 2118.

Place	Date	Hour	Summary of Events and Information	Remarks and references to Appendices
PAS	11/12/15		Morning Office and visited [illegible] (?). Afternoon. Office & finished A.F. W 3000 (?) weekly returns & got all correspondence up to date.	[initials]
"	12/12/15		Sunday – Morning Office and to see A.D.V.S. 48th Division – Afternoon to see D.D.V.S. 3rd Army –	[initials]
"	13/12/15		Morning – To M.V.S. to inspect cases for evacuation. Afternoon – To 37th Div Train	[initials]
"	14/12/15		Morning – To HENU to see another suspicious case of Glanders in A/125 Bde – Afternoon – Office	[initials]
"	15/12/15		Morning – To HENU and D.D.V.S. who came over to see the suspicious case – Afternoon to 37th Div Train to inspect [illegible] of 37th Reserve Park which arrived yesterday – and picked out 18 cases of Mange from them –	[initials]
"	16/12/15		Morning To HENU and on to GAUDIEMPRE to instruct Lieut Richardson in the Palpebral Test – Afternoon To 37th Div Train & Office –	[initials]
"	17/12/15		Morning To GAUDIEMPRE & HENU – met D.D.V.S. at the latter place – destroyed and [illegible] on P.M.E. a (?) case of Glanders and visited 37th Div Train – Afternoon conference of V.O.s –	[initials]
"	18/12/15		Morning Interview with G.O.C. on the subject of Glanders – Afternoon ~~[illegible]~~ & Office	[initials]
"	19/12/15		Sunday – Morning & Afternoon Office – Completed A.F. A 2000 – weekly Returns & got all correspondence up to date –	[initials]
"	20/12/15		Morning – Office and to M.V.S. to inspect cases for evacuation – Afternoon – Visited 37th Div Train – Evening – Office.	[initials]

Instructions regarding War Diaries and Intelligence Summaries are contained in F. S. Regs., Part II. and the Staff Manual respectively. Title pages will be prepared in manuscript.

WAR DIARY
or
INTELLIGENCE SUMMARY.
(Erase heading not required.)

Army Form C. 2118.

Place	Date	Hour	Summary of Events and Information	Remarks and references to Appendices
PAS	1/12/15		Returned from leave after having been delayed a day at Folkestone owing to the cross Channel Service being suspended – Resumed duties of A.D.V.S. from Capt. J.L.C. Jones A.V.C.	[illegible]
"	2/12/15		Morning – To La Couture to see D/123 Bde where animals are reported to be losing condition – Interviewed OC Bde – Saw unit and found standings very backward and horses generally neglected. Afternoon – Office.	[illegible]
"	3/12/15		Morning – To 7th Corps HQ to see R E expert on Horse standings – afternoon took D.D.R. on to see 37th DAC who are still very backward in their standings also – Afternoon Office & conference of V.O.	[illegible]
"	4/12/15		Morning – To M.V.S. and inspected the animals for evacuation – Afternoon Office.	[illegible]
"	5/12/15		Sunday – Morning – To 37th Div Train – Afternoon – Office, visit from Capt Jones and arranged to let him go on leave on the 8th inst.	[illegible]
"	6/12/15		Morning Office – Afternoon – G.O.C. Division inspected the 28th Mobile Vety Section, and expressed himself very pleased at everything he saw –	[illegible]
"	7/12/15		Morning – Visited 37th Div Train & 16 Bde R.G.A. – Afternoon Office	[illegible]
"	8/12/15		Morning – Office & visited 37th Div Train – Afternoon – Office	[illegible]
"	9/12/15		Morning – Office – visited D/126 Bde HQ RFA – Standings still very backward. Horses losing condition	[illegible]
"	10/12/15		Morning. Inspection D.H.Q. animals & office. Afternoon – Office & conference of V.O.s.	[illegible]

T2134. Wt. W708–776. 500000. 4/15. Sir J. C. & S.

Instructions regarding War Diaries and Intelligence Summaries are contained in F. S. Regs., Part II. and the Staff Manual respectively. Title Pages will be prepared in manuscript.

WAR DIARY
or
INTELLIGENCE SUMMARY
(Erase heading not required.)

Army Form C. 2118

Place	Date	Hour	Summary of Events and Information	Remarks and references to Appendices
PAS.	30/1/16		Sunday. Morning. Office and went out to look ~~out~~ for a suitable place for the M.V.S in case they have to move – went on to M.V.S and in the afternoon O.C. Section and self went out again in search of a suitable place and a little small farm near GRINCOURT – afternoon Office and wrote to D.D.V.S. 3rd Army and ~~asked~~ asked him to try and arrange for the M.V.S. to be left at MONDICOURT and if possible to get the Army Commander to come and inspect the place himself – and judge the matter on its own merits – ~~[illegible]~~ G.O.C. 37 Division has already moved in the matter but 7th Corps say we must go –	[illegible]
	31/1/16		Morning. Office and to Mondicourt and GRINCOURT to see about new Billets for the Section – M.V.S. evacuated and discharged all their cases today, pending having to vacate their billet on the 2-2-16. Afternoon. Office –	[illegible]

W. A. [illegible]. Major
A.D.V.S. 37th Division

1875 Wt. W593/826 1,000,000 4/15 J.B.C. & A. A.D.S.S./Forms/C. 2118.

Instructions regarding War Diaries and Intelligence Summaries are contained in F. S. Regs., Part II. and the Staff Manual respectively. Title Pages will be prepared in manuscript.

WAR DIARY
or
INTELLIGENCE SUMMARY
(Erase heading not required.)

Army Form C. 2118

Place	Date	Hour	Summary of Events and Information	Remarks and references to Appendices
PAS	24/1/16		Morning Office and to Mobile Vety Section. Afternoon – To SARTON to interview Civil Veterinary Surgeon M DELAPORTE who has been placed in charge of the horses care belonging to civilians in this area.	[illegible]
"	25/1/16		Morning Office and to HENU and inspected lines of the 125 Bde R.F.A. Afternoon – Office.	[illegible]
"	26/1/16		Morning Office and to 37th Divisional Train – Afternoon Office	[illegible]
"	27/1/16		Morning Office and to GAUDIEMPRE to see 16 Bde R G A & A/126 Bde. Afternoon Office and received message that D.V.S. was coming here tomorrow –	[illegible]
"	28/1/16		Morning Office – D.V.S. arrived at 11.30 AM. Took him to see the G.O.C. then on to GAUDIEMPRE where interviewed Lieut. Richardson regarding recent outbreak of Mange in B/126 Bde – after which he inspected the Horse Standings of the 9th & 14th Heavy Batteries 16th Bde R G A & A/126 Bde. all of which he was greatly pleased with. Thence to the 28th Mobile Vety Section with which he was very pleased – he said it was the best site for a M.V.S. he had seen and that it was the best M.V.S. he had seen – and he congratulated the OC Captain Jones and the Senior NCO Serg. Ford – Evening Office and received information that we may have vacate MONDICOURT to make room for the 4th Division –	[illegible]
"	29/1/16		Morning Office and to M.V.S. and selected the cases for evacuation – Evening Office –	[illegible]

1875 Wt. W593/826 1,000,000 4/15 J.B.C. & A. A.D.S.S./Forms/C. 2118.

Instructions regarding War Diaries and Intelligence Summaries are contained in F. S. Regs., Part II. and the Staff Manual respectively. Title Pages will be prepared in manuscript.

WAR DIARY
or
INTELLIGENCE SUMMARY
(Erase heading not required.)

Army Form C. 2118

Place	Date	Hour	Summary of Events and Information	Remarks and references to Appendices
PAS	17 1/16	–	Morning to FAMECHON with Lieut Sheffield handed over charge of Yorkshire Dragoons to him and finished their Mallein Testing – Afternoon. Office & Bacteriological work.	[illegible]
"	18 1/16		Morning Office – Afternoon. Office & Bacteriological work	[illegible]
"	19 1/16		Morning to LAHERLIERE to inspect 1/1 Kent Heavy Battery – and on to LA COUCHIE to see 123 Bde R.F.A. – Afternoon to 124 Bde and inspected AC/124 Bde for skin disease they have a lot of animals suffering from lice & Mange – without V.O. to send me some scrapings – Evening Office	[illegible]
"	20 1/16		Morning to St AMAND + HENU to see various cases – in 111th Inf Bde & C/125 Bde Afternoon – Office –	[illegible]
"	21 1/16		Morning. Office – Afternoon. Office	[illegible]
"	22 1/16		Morning. Office & to FAMECHON to see some suspicious skin case in Yorkshire Dragoons – afterwards on to Mobile Vety Section inspected the animals for evacuation – and spent the whole afternoon there going into things in the Office.	[illegible]
"	23 1/16		Sunday. Morning. Office. Afternoon Office Got Mobile Return finished & all correspondence up to date –	[illegible]

Instructions regarding War Diaries and Intelligence Summaries are contained in F. S. Regs., Part II. and the Staff Manual respectively. Title Pages will be prepared in manuscript.

WAR DIARY
or
INTELLIGENCE SUMMARY
(Erase heading not required.)

Army Form C. 2118

Place	Date	Hour	Summary of Events and Information	Remarks and references to Appendices
PAS	9/1/16		Sunday – Morning. Office – finished A.F. A2000. Afternoon to LA COUCHIE and onto St AMAND to see OC 126 Bde re Mange in B/126. – Received another 1500 doses of Mallein so shall be able to continue Testing which have been held up since before Xmas for want of Mallein –	[illegible]
"	10/1/16		Morning. Office & To 37th Div Train (Mallein Testing) afternoon. Started Mallein Testing D.H.Q	[illegible]
"	11/1/16		Morning – Office & To St AMAND, SOUASTRE & GAUDIEMPRE re Mange – afternoon – Continued Mallein D.H.Q re & Office.	[illegible]
"	12/1/16		Morning. Office & To Div Train south GAUDIEMPRE & HENU to inspect suspicious cases of Mange – afternoon – Mallein Testing. 49th Field Ambulance & R.E.	[illegible]
"	13/1/16		Morning – Office. Started Testing Pioneers – & continued with 37th Div Train. Afternoon. continued Testing D.H.Q. & Office.	[illegible]
"	14/1/16		Morning Office. To FAMECHON: started testing Yorkshire Dragoons – found 2 cases of Psoroptic Mange amongst civilian horses in the Bread Mill – Afternoon. Office re return of V.O.'s. Lieut Sheffield arrived vice Lt Pryor [illegible]	[illegible]
"	15/1/16		Morning Office & took Lieut Sheffield to 37th Div Train – Continued Testing there and left him working. Afternoon. To FAMECHON re Mange in the civilian horses. Office.	[illegible]
"	16/1/16		Sunday – Morning and To SOUASTRE with [illegible] – afternoon – To Mobile Vety Section and inspected cases for evacuation – Evening Office –	[illegible]

1875 Wt. W593/826 1,000,000 4/15 J.B.C. & A. A.D.S.S./Forms/C. 2118.

Instructions regarding War Diaries and Intelligence Summaries are contained in F. S. Regs., Part II. and the Staff Manual respectively. Title Pages will be prepared in manuscript.

WAR DIARY
or
INTELLIGENCE SUMMARY
(Erase heading not required.)

Army Form C. 2118

Place	Date	Hour	Summary of Events and Information	Remarks and references to Appendices
PAS.	1/1/16		Morning. Office – To ABBEVILLE for interview with D.V.S. on Glanders and Mallein Testing – Major Olver and Holiday both present – Spent the whole day there, and returned here at 6.30 pm. Office –	hmt
"	2/1/16		Sunday – morning Office and ~~[illegible]~~ finished off A.F. A 2000. Afternoon To M.V.S. and inspected animals for evacuation. Evening Office.	hmt
"	3/1/16		Morning. Office + To GAUDIEMPRE to inspect B/126 Bde and found a number of cases of Sarcoptic Mange. Took scrapings. and gave instructions for further isolation – Afternoon. Office	hmt
"	4/1/16		Morning. Office + To 37th Div Train. Afternoon. Office	hmt
"	5/1/16		Morning. Office + To GAUDIEMPRE re Mange B/126 Bde – Afternoon. Office	hmt
"	6/1/16		Morning. Office. + To 37th Div Train – [illegible] the BAZEQUE from the 124 Bde. Afternoon – Office.	hmt
"	7/1/16		Morning. Office and To FAMECHON to see Yorkshire Dragoons. then to M.V.S. to inspect animals for evacuation. – Afternoon. – Office. [illegible] of V.O.s.	hmt
"	8/1/16		Morning – To GAUDIEMPRE re Mange in B/126 Bde – Afternoon. Office	hmt

1875 Wt. W593/826 1,000,000 4/15 J.B.C. & A. A.D.S.S./Forms/C. 2118.

A.D.S. 37th Div.

Vol: 7

Instructions regarding War Diaries and Intelligence Summaries are contained in F. S. Regs., Part II. and the Staff Manual respectively. Title Pages will be prepared in manuscript.

Original

WAR DIARY
or
INTELLIGENCE SUMMARY
(Erase heading not required.)

Army Form C. 2118

Place	Date	Hour	Summary of Events and Information	Remarks and references to Appendices
PAS	19/2/16		Morning & afternoon. Office. Getting mobile returns completed & preparing for move.	[illegible]
"	20/2/16		Sunday. Morning Office. To GAUDIEMPRE to see [illegible] case. Visited M.V.S. Afternoon. D.D.R. came to inspect [illegible] case [illegible]. Evening. Office [illegible]	[illegible]
"	21/2/16		Morning. Moved to BAVINCOURT with D.H.Q. and called in at M.V.S. & Advanced Collecting Station en route. Afternoon. Inspected & fixed up new Office. Very cold	[illegible]
BAVINCOURT	22/2/16		Morning. Slight fall of snow. Office. and walked to LARBRET to see M.V.S. re [illegible] case for the Base. Afternoon. Office. More snow and very cold.	[illegible]
"	23/2/16		Morning. Office. Visited [illegible] at LA CAUCHIE [illegible] with V.O. [illegible]. Afternoon. Heavy fall of snow	[illegible]
"	24/2/16		Morning Inspected D.H.Q. Horses. Still snowing & very cold. Afternoon. [illegible] at La Cauchie [illegible] Bomb. 1 Horse killed & 4 wounded [illegible] which I had to destroy afterwards. [illegible] with D.H.Q. [illegible] one [illegible]. Evening. Office.	[illegible]
"	25/2/16		Morning. Office. Afternoon. Heavy snow fall. Office	
"	26/2/16		Morning. Office. [illegible] Returns and instructing a new clerk. [illegible] clerk [illegible].	[illegible]
"	27/2/16	Sunday	Morning. Office. Busy with Returns. Afternoon. Visited [illegible] of the Trenches which [illegible]	[illegible]
"	28/2/16		Morning. Visited Advanced Collecting Station. Afternoon. [illegible] and [illegible] at M.V.S. [illegible] case of evacuation. Evening. Office. Thawing fast.	[illegible]
"	29/2/16		Morning. Office. To LARBRET. Evacuation of animals from M.V.S. [illegible] To LA CAUCHIE [illegible] Bailleulmont. Afternoon & Evening. Office.	[illegible]

[illegible], Major, A.D.V.S. 37th Division

1875 Wt. W593/826 1,000,000 4/15 J.B.C. & A. A.D.S.S./Forms/C. 2118.

Army Form C. 2118

Instructions regarding War Diaries and Intelligence Summaries are contained in F. S. Regs., Part II. and the Staff Manual respectively. Title Pages will be prepared in manuscript.

WAR DIARY
or
INTELLIGENCE SUMMARY

(Erase heading not required.)

Place	Date	Hour	Summary of Events and Information	Remarks and references to Appendices
PAS.	11/2/16		Morning. Office and D.H.Q. accounts – Afternoon. Office conference of V.O.'s	WT
"	12/2/16		Morning. Visited LARBRET and prospected for a suitable place for the M.V.S. as this place will be our Railhead on and after the 18th inst. Saw some good farms, but am afraid there will be none available for the M.V.S.	WT
"	13/2/16		Sunday – Morning Office – Afternoon Office. Rode to St. Amand to see Lt White to give him instructions about moving to Bailleulmont	WT
"	14/2/16		Morning Office – Afternoon to BAVINCOURT and LARBRET with the French Liaison Officer to arrange about my Billet & Office at the former, and about a suitable place at the latter either for the M.V.S. or an Advanced Collecting Station.	
"	15/2/16		Morning – To GAUDIEMPRE to inspect some suspected skin cases in the 14th Battery R.G.A. at LA BAZIQUE FARM to see A.C./124 Bde. route POMMIER to see suspected skin case belonging to H.Q. 124 Bde. Afternoon Office	WT
"	16/2/16		Morning. Very heavy Rain Storms – To M.V.S. and find that the Shelters which are building are standing the storm very well. Afternoon with O.C. 37 Div Train to LARBRET to inspect Billets + Horse Standings	WT
"	17/2/16		Morning Office and to M.V.S. Afternoon with O.C. 2? M.V.S. to LARBRET and fixed on a billet and suitable place for a Detachment from the Section with the Horse Ambulance – To form an Advanced Collecting Station and Veterinary Aid Post –	WT
"	18/2/16		Morning Office – Afternoon. Office & Bacteriology – examining skin scrapings	
"	19/2/16		Morning to La Herlière & La Cauchie to see 1/1 Kent Bty R.G.A. & 123rd Bde R.F.A. Advanced Collecting Station established at LARBRET. Afternoon went on to 124 Bde. Inspected A.C./124 Bde. for skin Disease. [illegible] and Leg Mange – instructed V.O. to send me some more scrapings – Evening Office	WT WT

1875 Wt. W593/826 1,000,000 4/15 J.B.C. & A. A.D.S.S./Forms/C. 2118.

Instructions regarding War Diaries and Intelligence Summaries are contained in F. S. Regs., Part II. and the Staff Manual respectively. Title Pages will be prepared in manuscript.

Army Form C. 2118

WAR DIARY
or
INTELLIGENCE SUMMARY
(Erase heading not required.)

Place	Date	Hour	Summary of Events and Information	Remarks and references to Appendices
PAS	4/2/16		Morning. Inspected D.H.Q. animals and 49th Field Ambulance. Afternoon – Office and conference of V.O's. Evening inspected case of Suspected Mange in D/126 Bde – wire to V.O. i/c and report to Staff Captain R.A.	W.A.T.
"	5/2/16		Morning inspected D/126 Bde for Mange. and picked out 3 slightly Suspicious cases plus some other lame & debility cases for evacuation. and submitted report to Staff Captain R.A. – Afternoon to M.V.S. who are getting on well with their Shelters. Evening. Office –	W.A.T.
"	6/2/16		Sunday – Morning Office – Completed Weekly Returns. &c. – Afternoon to M.V.S. and inspected cases for evacuation.	W.A.T.
"	7/2/16		Morning. To 124 Bde to see B/124. also looked at A/124 and found that they had 8 Horses isolated under suspicion for Mange – instructed V.O. i/c to send me fresh scrapings from these. and take all precautions. Afternoon Office.	W.A.T.
"	8/2/16		To 37th D.A.C. to inquire into complaint re 45 horses reported to be lame & unfit out of lot sent to 46th Division and sent Lieut. Sheffield to Norman at once to inspect the animals himself.	
"	9/2/16		Morning. Office. Afternoon to A/124 Bde & inspected Battery for Mange – picked out 6 more suspicious cases and took fresh scrapings from other isolated cases – but could not isolate the Parasite. Gave instructions for 12 horses to be evacuated as Suspicious – & 4 for debility –	W.A.T.
"	10/2/16		Morning. Office. Afternoon to M.V.S. to inspect cases for evacuation – Afternoon. Office –	W.A.T.

Instructions regarding War Diaries and Intelligence Summaries are contained in F. S. Regs., Part II. and the Staff Manual respectively. Title Pages will be prepared in manuscript.

WAR DIARY
or
INTELLIGENCE SUMMARY
(Erase heading not required.)

Army Form C. 2118

Place	Date	Hour	Summary of Events and Information	Remarks and references to Appendices
PAS	1 2/16		Morning. To MONDICOURT to see OC 28 M.V.S. regarding the orders which have been received about the move of the Section. After which OC M.V.S. came with me to D.H.Q. to see R.E. and OC Timber Depot re material for their new Billets & shelters. Afternoon Office.	W.T.
"	2 2/16		Morning, ~~[illegible]~~ 28 M.V.S. vacated their billet at MONDICOURT and move to a small farm at GRINCOURT. I visited their billets at MONDICOURT after they had left to see that they had left them clean and in good order and I then visited them at their new Billet and found them busy cleaning out the place and all working well. A what is a very poor place after what they have left and which has been taken over by the 1st Batt. Royal Warwicks (4th Divn). Afternoon visited the Section again and arranged about transport to carry Timber and material which they are getting to make new shelters. In the morning I also visited HENU and inspected D/121 Bde. and a suspicious case of Mange which they have. Animal and contacts are isolated - and found two very suspicious [illegible] Sarcoptic Mange. Have the case further isolated. Went round the other horses - and gave necessary instructions. Evening Office and correspondence work.	W.T.
	3 2/16		Morning Office and to M.V.S. & 37th Div. Train. Afternoon. Office and to M.V.S. again.	W.T.

1875 Wt. W593/826 1,000,000 4/15 J.B.C. & A. A.D.S.S./Forms/C. 2118.

Instructions regarding War Diaries and Intelligence Summaries are contained in F. S. Regs., Part II. and the Staff Manual respectively. Title Pages will be prepared in manuscript.

WAR DIARY
or
INTELLIGENCE SUMMARY
(Erase heading not required.)

Army Form C. 2118

Place	Date	Hour	Summary of Events and Information	Remarks and references to Appendices
BAVINCOURT	1/3/16		Morning. Office – & to GAUDIEMPRE to see some skin cases in the [illegible]/126 Bde. Also visited the 1/2nd Home Cy. Battery who are moving tomorrow – They have 3 horses to be left behind suffering from Ulcerated [illegible] and 1 horse to be destroyed for Traumatic Arthritis.	
			Afternoon. Office – Busy with Monthly Returns.	[initials]
"	2/3/16		Morning. Office. To BASSEUX, BAILLEULVAL, BAILLEULMONT. Afternoon. Office & [illegible] D.H.Q. animals.	[initials]
"	3/3/16		Morning. Office, Round D.H.Q. animals & visited 132 Co. R.E. (A.T.) Afternoon – Conference of V.O.'s & Office.	[initials]
"	4/3/16		Morning. Heavy fall of snow which continued all day – Morning to AUTHIEULE with D.A.A.Q.M.G. to inspect the 3 Brigade M.G. Companies which have just arrived from England for the Division & [illegible] them on the march to their respective Brigades and that these [illegible] were in a very bad state. [illegible] of the 112th Co and with the assistance of some shoeing smiths from the 4th Div. (who were close by) [illegible] about 20 others put on and these [illegible] – Afternoon. Office.	
"	5/3/16		Sunday – Morning. Office – All [illegible] weekly Returns sent off.	[initials]
"	6/3/16		Snowing & thawing all day – Morning. Office. & to Advanced Collecting Station at LARBRET to inspect animals for evacuation – Afternoon attended G.O.C.'s Inspection of New Machine Gun Companies and also visited BASSEUX.	[initials]
"	7/3/16		Morning. Office and to visited Advanced Collecting Station at LARBRET. Afternoon. Office and to LARBRET Station to see M.V.S. evacuating cases – afterwards to the O.C. 55 Div Supply Column and arranged with him for the Detail 2 [illegible] to remain at LARBRET.	[initials]

1875 Wt. W593/826 1,000,000 4/15 J.B.C. & A. A.D.S.S./Forms/C. 2118.

Army Form C. 2118

Instructions regarding War Diaries and Intelligence Summaries are contained in F. S. Regs., Part II. and the Staff Manual respectively. Title Pages will be prepared in manuscript.

WAR DIARY
or
INTELLIGENCE SUMMARY
(Erase heading not required.)

Place	Date	Hour	Summary of Events and Information	Remarks and references to Appendices
BAVINCOURT	8/3/16		Morning. Office and attending to animals at D.H.Q. Afternoon. To BARLY & SAULTY. Evening. Office.	[initials]
"	9/3/16		Morning. Office and attending to animals at D.H.Q. Afternoon to 37 Div Train M.V.S.	
"	10/3/16		Morning Office – Afternoon. Conference of V.O.'s & Office	[initials]
"	11/3/16		Morning. To GAUDIEMPRE and inspected 1/1 Lowland Bty R.G.A. – Visit from A.D.V.S. 55th Division. Afternoon. To [illegible] to see Capt Shepherd A.V.C. and wrote Le Couchie to [illegible] and inform him that his leave had been sanctioned.	[initials]
"	12/3/16		Sunday. Morning. Office. Completed and Despatched Weekly Returns. Afternoon. Office.	[initials]
"	13/3/16		Morning To 4th Division HQ to see the A.D.V.S. re exchanging areas but missed him as he came over to see me. and went on to LARBRET & GRINCOURT to see an Advanced Collecting Station M.V.S. Billets. Afternoon visited these places myself and wired A.D.V.S. 4th Division to come and see me in the morning.	[initials]
"	14/3/16		Morning visit from A.D.V.S. 4th Division. Gave him all particulars about our area – as to where & what contagious & infectious Diseases we had had. and made arrangements to hand over the M.V.S. Billets and visit his M.V.S. tomorrow – Afternoon. Office.	[initials]
"	15/3/16		Morning – Office Afternoon to LUCHEUX and on to GROUCHES to meet A.D.V.S. [illegible] Division and arranged to take over their M.V.S. at this village – It is a dirty untidy place but I think we should be able to make something of it – On return [illegible] message that [illegible] had been taken	[initials] 1.50 [illegible] with Trans 104 [illegible]

1875 Wt. W593/826 1,000,000 4/15 J.B.C. & A. A.D.S.S./Forms/C. 2118.

Instructions regarding War Diaries and Intelligence Summaries are contained in F. S. Regs., Part II. and the Staff Manual respectively. Title Pages will be prepared in manuscript.

WAR DIARY
or
INTELLIGENCE SUMMARY
(Erase heading not required.)

Army Form C. 2118

Place	Date	Hour	Summary of Events and Information	Remarks and references to Appendices
BAVINCOURT	16 3/16		Morning – Arranged to take over Camp Commandant's Duties for 4 days – while he went on to the next place to make all arrangements for our arrival – Received message from OC 50 Field Ambulance that Lieut. J M White died at HENU this morning – Went there at once saw OC 50 Field Ambulance and arranged about funeral which is at 4 P.M today – Reported the casualty to D.D.V.S 3rd Army by wire & Visited M.V.S on way back and arranged there to send a party to the funeral. Showed A.P.M.S round the Billets at the same time – Afternoon. Lieut. J M White's funeral – Evening Office and sent D.D.V.S full acct of the funeral and other arrangements which I had made – Afterwards wrote to Mrs White – full details –	Wmt.
"	17 3/16		Morning. Office and round D.H.Q. animals. Afternoon. To M.V.S to see cases for evacuation. Evening Office.	Wmt.
"	18 3/16		Morning. Office – Afternoon to LARBRET to see about evacuations which are taking place today. Afterwards on to LA CAUCHIE to see Capt Sheffield – on return had visit from Lt Lazenby who is taking over Vety charge of the 16th Bde R.G.A. – Evening Busy in Camp Commandant's Office	Wmt.
"	19 3/16	Sunday	Morning. Office – Finished off weekly Returns – Afternoon Packed up Office & made all arrangements for move to LUCHEUX tomorrow –	Wmt.
"	20 3/16		Morning – Saw all kits D.H.Q loaded and Billets cleaned – marched the D.H.Q wagons to LUCHEUX. Afternoon – Fixed up my Office. Visited the M.V.S at GROUCHES – where they arrived today –	Wmt.

1875 Wt. W593/826 1,000,000 4/15 J.B.C. & A. A.D.S.S./Forms/C. 2118.

Army Form C. 2118

Instructions regarding War Diaries and Intelligence Summaries are contained in F. S. Regs., Part II. and the Staff Manual respectively. Title Pages will be prepared in manuscript.

WAR DIARY
or
INTELLIGENCE SUMMARY
(Erase heading not required.)

Place	Date	Hour	Summary of Events and Information	Remarks and references to Appendices
LUCHEUX.	21 3/16		Morning. Office - Afternoon to M.V.S. and on to see 48th Field Ambulance. 4th Pioneers - Evening. Office	[illegible]
"	22 3/16		Morning. Round D.H.Q. and [illegible] to Office. Afternoon. Office.	[illegible]
"	23 3/16		Morning. Visited 110 Inf. Bde. No. 2 Coy A.S.C. 41 F.A. & Pioneers - Afternoon Office	[illegible]
"	24 3/16		Morning. Visited 111 " " & No. 3 Co. A.S.C. Afternoon Office. Snowing & very cold all day -	[illegible]
"	25 3/16		Morning. Office. Visited M.V.S. & 49 Field Ambulance - Afternoon Office	[illegible]
"	26 3/16		Sunday - Morning & Afternoon Office. Evening to M.V.S.	[illegible]
"	27 3/16		Morning - Motored in to see to Captain Tom & Sheffield. Afternoon. Office	[illegible]
"	28 3/16		Morning - To Railhead to see M.V.S. evacuating, and on to see No. 3 Co. Div. Train & 48th Field Ambulance - Afternoon Office and to M.V.S.	[illegible]
"	29 3/16		Morning to MILLY to see No. 3 Bridging Train. Which has just arrived to [illegible] to be attached to the Division. but found most of the horses out - so arranged to [illegible] tomorrow - Back to LUCHEUX early to meet Commander-in-Chief who visited the Division today - He asked me how the Horses of the Division were and if I was in favour of clipping - I said "yes" Trace High. Afternoon - To [illegible] - St LEGER to see 110th Infantry Brigade -	[illegible]

1875 Wt. W593/826 1,000,000 4/15 J.B.C. & A. A.D.S.S./Forms/C. 2118.

Instructions regarding War Diaries and Intelligence Summaries are contained in F. S. Regs., Part II. and the Staff Manual respectively. Title Pages will be prepared in manuscript.

WAR DIARY
or
INTELLIGENCE SUMMARY
(Erase heading not required.)

Army Form C. 2118

Place	Date	Hour	Summary of Events and Information	Remarks and references to Appendices
LUCHEUX	30/3/16		Morning. Visited No 3 Coy 37 Div Train at BREVILLERS & 48 Field Ambulance at Le SOUICH. Afternoon. Office and inspected Right Half No 3 Coy Bridging Train which is now attached to the Division.	W.A.T.
"	31/3/16		Morning. Visited 111th Inf. Bde at SUS St LEGER. Afternoon. Office and conference of V.O.s.	W.A.T.

1-4-1916

W.A. Tatlin. Major
A.D.V.S. 37th Division

1875 Wt. W593/826 1,000,000 4/15 J.B.C. & A. A.D.S.S./Forms/C. 2118.

ADVS 37 Div

Army Form C. 2118

Vol 9

Instructions regarding War Diaries and Intelligence Summaries are contained in F. S. Regs., Part II. and the Staff Manual respectively. Title Pages will be prepared in manuscript.

WAR DIARY
or
INTELLIGENCE SUMMARY
(Erase heading not required.)

Place	Date	Hour	Summary of Events and Information	Remarks and references to Appendices
LUCHEUX	28/4/16		Morning – Office & visited H.Q. Co. 151st Co. Div Train. 48th Field Ambulance & Bridging Train – Afternoon – Office and conference of V.O's. –	WAP
"	29/4/16		Morning. Office. Afternoon – Visit from D.D.V.S. & D.D.R. 3rd Army – Brought them to see the M.V.S. at GROUCHES, where they inspected some samples of debilitated horses recently sent in from the R.A. – Afterwards accompanied them to R.A. Lines, MONDICOURT where D.D.V.S. inspected horses of C/126 Bde. and D.D.R. dealt with some Remount Cases.	WAP
"	30/4/16		Sunday – Morning Office – Finished Weekly Returns and visited M.V.S. and inspected cases for evacuation –	WAP

1-5-1916

W. A. Pallin. Maj.
A.D.V.S. 37th Division

1875 Wt. W593/826 1,000,000 4/15 J.B.C. & A. A.D.S.S./Forms/C. 2118.

Instructions regarding War Diaries and Intelligence Summaries are contained in F. S. Regs., Part II. and the Staff Manual respectively. Title Pages will be prepared in manuscript.

WAR DIARY
or
INTELLIGENCE SUMMARY
(Erase heading not required.)

Army Form C. 2118

Place	Date	Hour	Summary of Events and Information	Remarks and references to Appendices
LUCHEUX	25/4/16		Morning - Office - Afternoon attended inspection of R.A. Horses by Corps Commander. Pointed out to him how well those horses looked which had been properly cared for as compared with those of C/126 Bde. which I maintained had not. B.G.R.A. became rather rude and personal and endeavoured to avoid the point at issue viz. who was responsible for the watering & feeding of the Horses.	[illegible]
"	26/4/16		Morning - Interview with G.O.C. Division and report to him what Corps Commander and myself thought of the Horses viz. that on the whole they looked well - in fact some Batteries looked very well and were a credit to any Army, but the others particularly C/126 Bde. the horses looked wretched & I made a formal complaint against the attitude which the B.G.R.A. had taken up. and the G.O.C. said he would speak to Gen Potter about it. Later Office and to GROUCHES and inspected A C/126 Bde. Afternoon - Inspected A C/125 Bde. and all the 124 Bde and picked out a number of Horses for evacuation.	[illegible]
"	27/4/16		Morning - Office - Afternoon. Inspected C & D 125 Bde. & A. & B & A C/126 Bde. and picked out a number of horses for evacuation -	[illegible]

Instructions regarding War Diaries and Intelligence Summaries are contained in F. S. Regs., Part II. and the Staff Manual respectively. Title Pages will be prepared in manuscript.

WAR DIARY
or
INTELLIGENCE SUMMARY
(Erase heading not required.)

Army Form C. 2118

Place	Date	Hour	Summary of Events and Information	Remarks and references to Appendices
LUCHEUX	19/4/16		Morning Office. Afternoon. Visited R A lines at MONDICOURT with G.O.C. Division & G.S.O. 1. – The lines were in a terrible state owing to the constant rain and the animals are rapidly losing condition from exposure to the cold winds, rain, and condition of their standings – so it was decided to ask G.O.C. 7th Corps if the 123rd Bde which are coming out of the line, may be billeted at GROUCHES which was eventually agreed to.	WT
"	20/4/16		Morning. Office. Visited H.Q. & No 4 Co. Div Train & 2nd Field Ambulance – Afternoon Office – another cold wet day	WT
"	21/4/16		Morning. Office. Lieut. JEWELL AVC arrived vice JONES to England. Afternoon. Inspection of 113 Inf Bde. Office & conference of V.O's. Put Lt Jewell up at Lucheux for the night.	WT
"	22/4/16		Morning. Office. Spent the whole morning going through papers and instructing Lieut. Jewell in his duties. Afternoon. completed inspection of 112 Inf Bde. another horribly cold wet day.	WT
"	23/4/16		Easter Sunday – Morning Office & completed weekly Returns. Afternoon. To M.V.S. and inspected cases for evacuation.	WT
"	24/4/16		Morning Office. Visited R A lines at PAS & inspected C/126 Bde. whose horses are still in very poor condition – 22 again to be evacuated at once. Made special report to D.H.Q. about this unit – copy to D.D.V.S. 3rd Army	WT

1875 Wt. W593/826 1,000,000 4/15 J.B.C. & A. A.D.S.S./Forms/C. 2118.

Instructions regarding War Diaries and Intelligence Summaries are contained in F. S. Regs., Part II. and the Staff Manual respectively. Title Pages will be prepared in manuscript.

WAR DIARY
or
INTELLIGENCE SUMMARY
(Erase heading not required.)

Army Form C. 2118

Place	Date	Hour	Summary of Events and Information	Remarks and references to Appendices
LUCHEUX	10/4/16		Morning Office – Gave Capt JONES final instruction about his duties as A.D.V.S. and fitted him out with necessary lists of British Army Forms. Special Circulars & forms used in this Office previous to his departure. Afternoon inspected 111th Inf Bde Transport with OC 37 Div Train – Afternoon to HUMBERCAMP and Lieut. St LEGER to inspect some Transport of 110th Inf Bde which are being sent to the Base.	WNT
"	11/4/16		Morning Office Afternoon Office. Very wet & blowing all day. –	WNT
"	12/4/16		Morning Office D.D.R. had an inspection of Remount cases for casting at my Office. Afternoon – To 112th Inf Bde and [illegible] very well.	WNT
"	13/4/16		Morning Office Visited 112 Inf Bde 4th Field Ambulance & No. 4 Co. Div Train. Afternoon Visited HQ C Div Train HQ 27 Reserve Park + Amm Transport. –	WNT
"	14/4/16		Morning Office. Weekly Returns – Afternoon – Office & Conference of V.O.s –	WNT
"	15/4/16		Morning – Office Weekly Returns. Afternoon. Office & To Yorkshire Dragoons.	WNT
"	16/4/16		Sunday. Morning – Office. Got Weekly Returns finished – Afternoon To M.V.S. inspected cases for evacuation	WNT
"	17/4/16		Morning Office & Board on Shoeing Smiths – Afternoon Visited 111th Inf Bde	WNT
"	18/4/16		Morning Office – Afternoon Office. Raining and very cold all day. –	WNT

1875 Wt. W593/826 1,000,000 4/15 J.B.C. & A. A.D.S.S./Forms/C. 2118.

Instructions regarding War Diaries and Intelligence Summaries are contained in F. S. Regs., Part II. and the Staff Manual respectively. Title Pages will be prepared in manuscript.

WAR DIARY
or
INTELLIGENCE SUMMARY
(Erase heading not required.)

Army Form C. 2118

Place	Date	Hour	Summary of Events and Information	Remarks and references to Appendices
LUCHEUX	1/4/16		Morning Visited 8th Lincolns – Afternoon Office.	W.S.T.
"	2/4/16		Sunday. Morning Office & got weekly Return off. Afternoon. To M.V.S. inspected cases for evacuation	W.S.T.
"	3/4/16		Morning. Office. Visited HALLOY, GRENAS, MONDICOURT & PAS. Saw R.F.A. Bde & D.A.C. moving into their Rest Camp & Billets. Afternoon Office.	W.S.T.
"	4/4/16		Morning. Office. Visited No 2 Co Div Train, 48th F.A. 9th Lincolns & 110th Inf Bde. – Afternoon. Office.	W.S.T.
"	5/4/16		Morning Office Visited 110th Inf Bde. – Afternoon. Office.	W.S.T.
"	6/4/16		Morning. Office Inspected 110th Inf Machine Gun Co 6th 7th & 9th Lincolns with G.O.C. Brigade – afternoon visited Bridging Train (1/4 No 3 Co) Afternoon. Visited 111th Inf Bde. No 3 Co Div Train. 9th North Stafford & 1?3 Co. R.E.	W.S.T.
"	7/4/16		Morning. Office. To Railhead to see M.V.S. evacuating cases. Afternoon visited 48th Field Ambulance 1?? Co Div Train & No ? Co. ditto. Afternoon. Office. & conference of V.O.s	W.S.T.
"	8/4/16		Morning Office. – Afternoon. Office & to 110th Inf Bde. Evening wire directing Capt JONES to hand over to take over duties of A.D.V.S. of a Division.	W.S.T.
"	9/4/16		<u>Sunday</u> Morning Office Got weekly Return finished – Afternoon To M.V.S. inspected cases for evacuation and to RADBART to make inquiries about a reported outbreak of Foot & Mouth Disease.	W.S.T.

1875 Wt. W593/826 1,000,000 4/15 J.B.C. & A. A.D.S.S./Forms/C. 2118.

ADVS Vol 10

Army Form C. 2118

Instructions regarding War Diaries and Intelligence Summaries are contained in F. S. Regs., Part II. and the Staff Manual respectively. Title Pages will be prepared in manuscript.

WAR DIARY
or
INTELLIGENCE SUMMARY
(Erase heading not required.)

Place	Date	Hour	Summary of Events and Information	Remarks and references to Appendices
BAVINCOURT	26/5/16		Morning Office - New Clerk arrived from the Base - and will require instruction in every detail from the very beginning as he knows nothing about this kind of work, and is very short-sighted. Afternoon - Conference of V.O.s - Commander-in-Chief paid another visit to D.H.Q and again interviewed each one of the Staff.	WAP
"	27/5/16		Morning Office - and also inspected No 2 Section 37 Remount Park - Afternoon Office - Finished Weekly Return -	WAP
"	28/5/16		Sunday - To M.V.S and inspected animals for evacuation - Afternoon visited Advanced Collecting Station - Evening. Feeling rather seedy so to bed early -	WAP
"	29/5/16		Morning - Still feeling rather seedy - M.O. ordered me to stay in bed - which I did not until midday - Afternoon - Did some Office work but am not feeling at all well -	WAP
"	30/5/16		Morning - Feeling somewhat better - so rode to Gouy to see A.D.V.S. 55 Div re orders about Red Horse but unfortunately missed him - Afternoon Office and to Railhead to see M.V.S. evacuating cases to the Base. Also visited Advanced Collecting Station where I am having some improvements made - Still feeling very seedy -	WAP
"	31/5/16		Still very seedy. M.O. ordered me to stay in bed	WAP

W A Pallin Major
A.D.V.S 37 Division

1875 Wt. W593/826 1,000,000 4/15 J.B.C. & A. A.D.S.S./Forms/C. 2118.

Instructions regarding War Diaries and Intelligence Summaries are contained in F. S. Regs., Part II. and the Staff Manual respectively. Title Pages will be prepared in manuscript.

WAR DIARY
or
INTELLIGENCE SUMMARY
(Erase heading not required.)

Army Form C. 2118

Place	Date	Hour	Summary of Events and Information	Remarks and references to Appendices
BAVINCOURT	14 5/16		Morning & afternoon office Checked returns and dispatched same to D.D.V.S. 3rd Army	A.A.P.
"	15 5/16		Afternoon - office	A.A.P.
"	16 5/16		Afternoon - office	A.A.P.
"	17 5/16		Afternoon - office	A.A.P.
"	18 5/16		Afternoon - office.	A.A.P.
"	19 5/16		Morning. Return from leave - Reported arrival and went through all the ~~office~~ correspondence that has taken place during my absence. Afternoon. Conference of V.O.: Office	W.S.T.
"	20 5/16		Morning - Office - Afternoon To 7th Corps H.Q.	W.S.T.
"	21 5/16		Sunday - Morning Office finished Weekly Return. Afternoon To 2 M.V.S.	W.S.T.
"	22 5/16		Morning. Office. Afternoon. To 112 Inf Bde. M.V.S. D.A.C.	W.S.T.
"	23 5/16		Morning. Office & To Advanced Collecting Station. No 4 Co. Div Train. Afternoon - To D.A.C to inspect ~~...~~ animals which are being transferred to Base & other Division	W.S.T.
"	24 5/16		Morning Inspected the re-constituted 37 Divisional Column. Afternoon Office	W.S.T.
"	25 5/16		Morning. Office - Afternoon To Divisional School -	W.S.T.

1875 Wt. W593/826 1,000,000 4/15 J.B.C. & A. A.D.S.S./Forms/C. 2118.

Instructions regarding War Diaries and Intelligence Summaries are contained in F. S. Regs., Part II. and the Staff Manual respectively. Title Pages will be prepared in manuscript.

WAR DIARY
or
INTELLIGENCE SUMMARY
(Erase heading not required.)

Army Form C. 2118

Place	Date	Hour	Summary of Events and Information	Remarks and references to Appendices
BAVINCOURT	6/5/16		Morning - Lieut [illegible] of 2[illegible] M.V.S. informed that he might take [illegible] to LONGCAMP - Visit from A.D.V.S. 55th Division and assisted him with 2 P.M.'s [illegible] microscopical work. Also took over all the various attached units from him - was also busy all day with returns and allotting V.O.'s duties in the new area.	[illegible]
"	7/5/16		Sunday - Morning Office - Completed weekly Returns - Afternoon to LARBRET to inspect cases being evacuated. Evening Office.	[illegible]
"	8/5/16		Morning - Office - Afternoon To M.V.S. Evening Office.	[illegible]
"	9/5/16		Morning - Office [illegible] Afternoon left for Boulogne en route to England on leave. Captain [illegible] of 2[illegible] M.V.S. will act as A.D.V.S. & Capt. [illegible] will be i/c of the Office and D.H.Q. [illegible] during my absence	[illegible]
"	10/5/16		To office in afternoon. Reported that I had taken over my duties to "Q" staff. Dealt with correspondence & indents.	A.A.P.
"	11/5/16		To office in afternoon.	A.A.P.
"	12/5/16		Afternoon - office. Weekly conference of V.O.'s	A.A.P.
"	13/5/16		Afternoon - office	A.A.P.

1875 Wt. W593/826 1,000,000 4/15 J.B.C. & A. A.D.S.S./Forms/C. 2118.

Army Form C. 2118

Instructions regarding War Diaries and Intelligence Summaries are contained in F. S. Regs., Part II. and the Staff Manual respectively. Title Pages will be prepared in manuscript.

WAR DIARY
or
INTELLIGENCE SUMMARY
(Erase heading not required.)

Place	Date	Hour	Summary of Events and Information	Remarks and references to Appendices
LUCHEUX	1-5-16		Morning Office. Visited 112th Inf Bde. H.Q. & No. 4 Coy 37th Div Train. Afternoon. Office.	[illegible]
"	2-5-16		Morning. Visited M.V.S. and gave OC amended instructions re move. Afternoon to BAVINCOURT to see A.D.V.S. 4th Div. and onto GOUY to see A.D.V.S. 55th Div. Interviewed [illegible] him. then to SAULTY to see his M.V.S. with regard to letting me [struck out] Billet for the 28 M.V.S.	[illegible]
"	3-5-16		Morning moved Office from LUCHEUX to BAVINCOURT. Visited 4th M.V.S. at GROUCHES and 28th M.V.S. at GRINCOURT en route. Afternoon. Office. To GOUY to see A.D.V.S. 55th Div but he was out again. [struck out]	[illegible]
BAVINCOURT	4-5-16		Morning visited GOUY. Had interview with A.D.V.S. 55th Division and visited his Section at SAULTY with a view to letting me [struck out] Billet for the 28 M.V.S. Afternoon. To COURTRELLE to see if there was anything better in that direction & back via LARBRET.	[illegible]
"	5-5-16		Morning Office. Inspected A & B Batteries 125th Bde. Water Troughs at LARBRET which I found were out of order. Stand-Pipe is injured - the tubing badly. Reported to D.H.Q. at once. CRE informed. Afternoon - Office conference of V.O.'s - Afternoon to SONCAMP FARM with OC 28 M.V.S. and decided to send M.V.S. there instead of SAULTY. (Division D.H.Q. agree.) with A.V. [illegible] [struck out] there [illegible] LARBRET	[illegible]

Instructions regarding War Diaries and Intelligence Summaries are contained in F. S. Regs., Part II. and the Staff Manual respectively. Title Pages will be prepared in manuscript.

WAR DIARY
or
INTELLIGENCE SUMMARY
(Erase heading not required.)

ADVS

Army Form C. 2118

37 DW

Vol. 11

June

Place	Date	Hour	Summary of Events and Information	Remarks and references to Appendices
BAVINCOURT	26/6/16		Morning & afternoon Office	[illegible]
"	27/6/16		Morning & afternoon Inspecting 110th Infantry Bde. Transport	[illegible]
"	28/6/16		Morning Inspected 9th North Staffords – afternoon No 2 ~~R~~ Sectn. Remount Park. & office	[illegible]
"	29/6/16		Morning Inspected 111th Infantry Transport – afternoon 112th Infantry Bde Transport	[illegible]
"	30/6/16		Morning – Inspected some newly arrived Remounts belonging to 37th Div Column – and also visited Advanced Collecting Station afternoon – Office & Conference of V.O's	[illegible]

1st July 1916

W. A. Pallin. Major
A.D.V.S. 37th Division

1875 Wt. W593/826 1,000,000 4/15 J.B.C. & A. A.D.S.S./Forms/C. 2118.

WAR DIARY
or
INTELLIGENCE SUMMARY
(Erase heading not required.)

Army Form C. 2118

Instructions regarding War Diaries and Intelligence Summaries are contained in F. S. Regs., Part II. and the Staff Manual respectively. Title Pages will be prepared in manuscript.

Place	Date	Hour	Summary of Events and Information	Remarks and references to Appendices
BAVINCOURT	13/6/16		Morning – To LARBRET and LATTERLIERE – Afternoon inspected 123rd Bde R.F.A.	W.R.T.
"	14/6/16		Morning – Office To LARBRET and LATTERLIERE – Afternoon to Advanced Collecting Station and Railhead to see M.H. evacuating cars –	W.R.T.
"	15/6/16		Morning. Office. Lieut. J. H. YATES arrived – Took him over to LA COUCHIE. fixed him up with Groom. Horse & Billet. Put him in charge of the 124 Bde etc. – Afternoon. he attended at my Office for instruction	W.R.T.
"	16/6/16		Morning – Inspected 3 Battns 124 Bde. Afternoon Office & Conference of V.O.s.	W.R.T.
"	17/6/16		Morning – Completed Inspection of 124 Bde. Afternoon To judge at 55th Divn Horse Show	W.R.T.
"	18/6/16		Sunday. Morning. Office. Completed weekly Returns – Afternoon To judge at 55th Divn Horse Show	W.R.T.
"	19/6/16		Morning. Inspected 125 Bde – Afternoon Office	W.R.T.
"	20/6/16		Morning Inspected 126 Bde. Afternoon. Office.	W.R.T.
"	21/6/16		Morning ~~Inspected~~ and Afternoon – Inspected Echelon A. 37 Divl. Column. Evening. Office	W.R.T.
"	22/6/16		Morning. Inspected B. Echelon. 37 Divl. Column. Afternoon. Office –	W.R.T.
"	23/6/16		Morning – To LARBRET & LATTERLIERE – Afternoon Office. & Conference of V.O.s –	W.R.T.
"	24/6/16		Morning – Inspected 123rd Bde – Afternoon. Office –	W.R.T.
"	25/6/16		Sunday – Morning Office – Finished off weekly Returns – Afternoon To Advanced Collecting Station – and Railhead to see M.H. evacuating. Afterwards to 48th Field Ambulance to inspect three animals and another 2 Horses which were wounded by a Bomb this morning –	W.R.T.

Instructions regarding War Diaries and Intelligence Summaries are contained in F. S. Regs., Part II. and the Staff Manual respectively. Title Pages will be prepared in manuscript.

WAR DIARY
or
INTELLIGENCE SUMMARY
(Erase heading not required.)

Army Form C. 2118

Place	Date	Hour	Summary of Events and Information	Remarks and references to Appendices
BAVINCOURT	1/6/16		Major W. A. Pallin placed on sick list & removed to 48th Field Amb. at noon. On account of this received instructions at 9 a.m. to proceed to D.H.Q. to take over his duties. Occupied in office until 6 p.m.	A.A.P.
"	2/6/16		Office & held weekly conference of V.O's in afternoon	A.A.P.
"	3/6/16		Office & preparing weekly returns for D.D.V.S. 3rd Army	A.A.P.
"	4/6/16		Heavy rain. Office in afternoon. Visited 28 Mobile Section Advanced Collecting Station in evening.	A.A.P.
"	5/6/16		Office. Inspected D/123 R.F.A. owing to V.O. having reported a case of suspected psoroptic mange	A.A.P.
"	6/6/16		Examined skin scrapings. Unable to find parasite in scrapings from horse of D/123 but evacuated it as clinically suspicious	A.A.P.
"	7/6/16		Five cases of suspected mange reported. Examined scrapings & inspected units concerned	A.A.P.
"	8/6/16		Heavy rain. Office. Visited Major Pallin at 48th Field Ambulance	A.A.P.
"	9/6/16		Inspected 147 (A.T.) Coy R.E. in morning. Afternoon office and held weekly conference of V.O's	A.A.P.
"	10/6/16		Morning - Office - Germans shelled our Railhead and amongst other casualties - Capt. W. L. Sheffield was wounded	
"	"		Afternoon - Office. Conference of V.O's - Returned to duty and took over duties again from Captain Page -	W.A.P.
"	11/6/16		Sunday - Morning - Office. Finished off weekly Returns - Afternoon - Office - Brought everything up to date -	W.A.P.
"	12/6/16		Morning. Office - Afternoon - To Advanced Collecting Station - M.V.S. and inspected cases for evacuation -	W.A.P.

1875 Wt. W593/826 1,000,000 4/15 J.B.C. & A. A.D.S.S./Forms/C. 2118.

Army Form C. 2118

Instructions regarding War Diaries and Intelligence Summaries are contained in F. S. Regs., Part II. and the Staff Manual respectively. Title Pages will be prepared in manuscript.

WAR DIARY
or
INTELLIGENCE SUMMARY

(Erase heading not required.)

Place	Date	Hour	Summary of Events and Information	Remarks and references to Appendices
BAVINCOURT	1.7.16		Morning – Office – Busy with Weekly Returns – Afternoon – Office + Took over duties of Camp Commandant temporarily in addition to my other duties –	W.P.
"	2.7.16		Sunday – Morning Office – Finished off Weekly Returns – Afternoon To 28 M.V.S. to warn them about the move. And went on to PAS to see Corps Camp Commandant, Re Billets for D.H.Q. –	W.P.
"	3.7.16		Morning – Office & To Pas re Billets – Afternoon To PAS again re Billets –	W.P.
"	4.7.16		Moved D.H.Q. Transport to PAS and fixed up everyone in their Billets & and 28 M.V.S. moved back to their old Billet at GRINCOURT.	W.P.
PAS	5.7.16		Morning – Office and completed some more details about Billets – Afternoon Handed over duties of Camp Commandant to Captain Mitford who has returned to D.H.Q.	W.P.
"	6.7.16		Morning Office – 110th 111th & 112th Inf Bde completed their transfer from the Divn today – and are being replaced by 102nd 103rd & 63rd Inf Bde – Afternoon To M.V.S. – & Office –	W.P.
"	7.7.16		Morning Inspected D.I. Horses – Afternoon To WARLUZEL to see 123rd Bde moving back into the line	W.P.
"	8.7.16		Morning – Inspected 102nd & 103rd Inf Bde. Transport – 63rd H.Q. Company 34 Divl Train. Afternoon. Office – D.D.V.S. arrived & went to see the 28th M.V.S. –	W.P.

1875 Wt. W593/826 1,000,000 4/15 J.B.C. & A. A.D.S.S./Forms/C. 2118.

Instructions regarding War Diaries and Intelligence Summaries are contained in F. S. Regs., Part II. and the Staff Manual respectively. Title Pages will be prepared in manuscript.

WAR DIARY
or
INTELLIGENCE SUMMARY
(Erase heading not required.)

Army Form C. 2118

Place	Date	Hour	Summary of Events and Information	Remarks and references to Appendices
BRYAS.	18/7/16		Morning - Visit from D.D.V.S. 1st Army - Afternoon to see some cases which have been left behind in Billets by troops on the march -	W.P.
"	19/7/16		Moved to LE COMTE'. Afternoon visited BEUGIN & HOUDAIN and decided on moving the M.V.S. to the 1st named village - good standing - water - an orchard - also privacy - later O.C. 2 M.V.S. came over & visited the Billet with me - and after getting permission from the Corps to move there - I sent O.C. written instructions to do so - as soon as possible -	W.P.
LE COMTE'	20/7/16		Morning & Afternoon. Office -	W.P.
"	21/7/16		Morning Office - Afternoon Office & to see M.V.S. who have moved into temporary Billets at HERMIN.	W.P.
"	22/7/16		Morning to PERNES to see horses arrived at 4th Corps School of Instruction and onto Division to see 102nd Inf Bde.	W.P.
"	23/7/16		Sunday - Morning & Afternoon. Office Sick & of Returns. Evening visited M.V.S. in their new Billet at BEUGIN	W.P.
"	24/7/16		Morning & Afternoon out round R.A. Wagon lines at CAUCOURT & GAUCHIN LEGAL who visited M.V.S. Evening. Office.	W.P.
"	25/7/16		Morning Office - Afternoon round part of new area	W.P.
"	26/7/16		Morning Office. Afternoon called on A.D.V.S. 47th Division - afterwards to FRESNICOURT to see site for M.V.S. which we are taking over -	W.P.

1875 Wt. W593/826 1,000,000 4/15 J.B.C. & A. A.D.S.S./Forms/C. 2118.

Instructions regarding War Diaries and Intelligence Summaries are contained in F. S. Regs., Part II. and the Staff Manual respectively. Title Pages will be prepared in manuscript.

WAR DIARY
or
INTELLIGENCE SUMMARY
(Erase heading not required.)

Army Form C. 2118

Place	Date	Hour	Summary of Events and Information	Remarks and references to Appendices
PAS.	9/7/16		Sunday – Morning Office. Busy with Weekly Returns – Afternoon. To GAUDIEMPRE to arrange about Billets for 2 Bdes of R.F.A. – Evening – Office – Got Returns all finished.	M.P.
"	10/7/16		Morning – Inspected 183rd Inf Bde + 18 N.F. Pioneers. Transport. Afternoon inspected B.T. Coy 3rd Pontoon Park. ~~[illegible]~~ for Mange – Evening. Office –	M.P.
"	11/7/16		Morning. Office – to GAUDIEMPRE to see 123rd Bde, 49th + 50th Field Ambulance. Afternoon Office –	M.P.
"	12/7/16		Morning to 28 M.V.S. – inspected cases for evacuation – Afternoon to Beaumetz & inspected H.Q + No 2 Section 27 Reserve Park – Afternoon – Office.	M.P.
"	13/7/16		Morning. Office – Afternoon to see A.D.V.S. 56th Division –	M.P.
"	14/7/16		Morning – To M.V.S. and 37 Div. Column – Afternoon Conference of V.O.'s – Later A.D.V.S. 56th Division called. Took him to see 28 M.V.S. and also visited his M.V.S. and arranged to hand over our Billet at GRINCOURT to him tomorrow –	M.P.
"	15/7/16		~~Moved~~ Morning Office & completed Weekly Returns – Afternoon moved to LIENCOURT. M.V.S. to BROUILLY.	M.P.
LIENCOURT	16/7/16		Sunday. Moved to BRYAS and joined 4th Corps. 1st Army – M.V.S. to CAUCOURT.	M.P.
BRYAS.	17/7/16		With O.C. Train round the area – visited Train Companies & Inf Transport. M.V.S.	M.P.

1875 Wt. W593/826 1,000,000 4/15 J.B.C. & A. A.D.S.S./Forms/C. 2118.

37 July

Army Form C. 2118

37 ADVS

Vol 12

WAR DIARY
or
INTELLIGENCE SUMMARY
(Erase heading not required.)

Instructions regarding War Diaries and Intelligence Summaries are contained in F. S. Regs., Part II. and the Staff Manual respectively. Title Pages will be prepared in manuscript.

Place	Date	Hour	Summary of Events and Information	Remarks and references to Appendices
LE COMTE'	27.7.16		Morning Office - Afternoon Office -	W.T.
"	28.7.16		Moved to CAMBLAIN L'ABBE' - Afternoon conference of V.O's. Then very bad Office so moved into Camp Commandant's Office -	W.T.
CAMBLAIN L'ABBE'	29.7.16		Morning out with A.A.Q.M.G. & gave a Veterinary lecture to some young Officers which have just joined the 103rd Infantry Bde. Afternoon to MONT. St. ELOI to see some Batteries in the forward area -	W.T.
"	30.7.16		Morning Office - Finished off weekly Returns - Afternoon to M.V.S.	W.T.
"	31.7.16		Morning Office - Afternoon to IV Corps H.Q. Evening Office -	W.T.

1st August 1916.

W.T. [illegible] Major
A.D.V.S. 37th Division

1875 Wt. W593/826 1,000,000 4/15 J.B.C. & A. A.D.S.S./Forms/C. 2118.

Instructions regarding War Diaries and Intelligence Summaries are contained in F. S. Regs., Part II. and the Staff Manual respectively. Title Pages will be prepared in manuscript.

WAR DIARY
or
INTELLIGENCE SUMMARY
(Erase heading not required.)

A. D. V. S
37th DIVISION

37 Army Form C. 2118

VOL 13

Place	Date	Hour	Summary of Events and Information	Remarks and references to Appendices
CAMBLAIN L'ABBE'	1/8/16	-	Morning & afternoon. D.D.V.S. 1st Army Inspection of R.A. Horses.	W.R.
"	2/8/16		" " " " " " Horses Mules.	W.R.
"	3/8/16		Morning office & to 103rd Inf. Bde H.Q. gave a lecture to some young officers & also visited the M.V.S. - Afternoon went to MONCHY-CAYEUX to see about a horse left there by another Division. Evening office.	W.R.
"	4/8/16		Morning inspection of D.H.Q animals - Afternoon office & conference of V.O's	W.R.
"	5/8/16		Morning office & visited M.V.S. Afternoon. office & finished off weekly returns.	W.R.
"	6/8/16		Sunday - Morning office. Afternoon to conference of A.D.V.S. at D.D.V.S. 1st Army office.	W.R.
"	7/8/16		Morning - My clerk taken to Hospital in order to be sent to the Base to have his eyes seen to. Inspected 102nd Inf Bde Transport. Afternoon. Inspected 103rd Inf Bde Transport.	W.R.
"	8/8/16		Morning Inspected 63rd Inf. Bde Transport - afternoon office.	W.R.
"	9/8/16		Morning Inspected some L.D Horses recently handed over to 37th Divl Train. Afternoon office.	W.R.
"	10/8/16		Morning Inspected 48th 49th & 50 Field Ambulance Transport - Afternoon office.	W.R.

1875 Wt. W593/826 1,000,000 4/15 J.B.C. & A. A.D.S.S./Forms/C. 2118.

Instructions regarding War Diaries and Intelligence Summaries are contained in F. S. Regs., Part II. and the Staff Manual respectively. Title Pages will be prepared in manuscript.

WAR DIARY
or
INTELLIGENCE SUMMARY
(Erase heading not required.)

Army Form C. 2118

Place	Date	Hour	Summary of Events and Information	Remarks and references to Appendices
CAMBLAIN L'Abbé	11 8/16		Morning - Office. Afternoon office & conference of V.O.s.	W.D.S.
"	12 8/16		Morning Office. Finished off weekly returns. Afternoon received instructions to proceed to Boulogne as D.D.V.S. Northern. Vice Lieut Col. W.D. Smith immediately & to hand over duties of A.D.V.S. 37th Divn to Capt. Rayne.	W.D.S.
"	13 8/16		Morning. Office. Conference of V.O.s & Handed over to Captain Rayne ~~[illegible]~~ Afternoon Visited the M.V.S. and left for Boulogne	W.D.S.
"		3 p.m.	Took over A.D.V.S.' duties from Major PALLIN and reported to that effect by wire to D.D.V.S. 1st Army	A.A.P.
"	14 8/16		Morning to railhead to see animals evacuated. Afternoon & evening office. Preparing to move next day. Drew up list of attached units for handing over to 9th Divn & re-posted veterinary officers. Visited R.A. Hdqrs.	A.A.P.
"	15 8/16		D.H.Q. moved to BRUAY marching at 9 a.m.	
BRUAY		3 p.m.	Arrived & arranged office. Was informed by 'Q' office that 37th Divl. R.A. would march to join VIth Corps 3rd Army on 17 inst. Resolved to send 3 V.O.'s & keep two back to do Divl. Infantry & other units. Sent operation orders to Capt. WADDELL to move with 37th Divl Column. Capt. J.A. STANFORD to go i/c of 125 & 126 Bdes & Lt. JEWELL i/c of 123 & 124 Bdes. Ordered Lt. YATES to hand over 124th Bde & await posting probably to 103rd Inf. Bde. Sent preliminary report to D.D.V.S. 1st Army & to Staff Captain 37th R.A.	A.A.P.

1875 Wt. W593/826 1,000,000 4/15 J.B.C. & A. A.D.S.S./Forms/C. 2118.

Army Form C. 2118

WAR DIARY
or
INTELLIGENCE SUMMARY
(Erase heading not required.)

Instructions regarding War Diaries and Intelligence Summaries are contained in F. S. Regs., Part II. and the Staff Manual respectively. Title Pages will be prepared in manuscript.

Place	Date	Hour	Summary of Events and Information	Remarks and references to Appendices
BRUAY.	16.8.16		Visited 124 + 125 Bdes. & 37th Divnl. Column in morning & gave final instructions to V.O's. Posted Lt. YATES to H.Q. Coy Divnl Train & divided units between Lt. & CAPT. HUSTON - the two remaining V.O's.	A.A.P.
"	17.8.16		Received message from Lt. YATES & S.O. in saying that Hdqrs. Coy Divnl. Train were going with R.A. & asking for further instructions. Sent word to him to stand fast & will probably post him to No 4 Sec. 37th Divnl. Column at HOUVELIN who are remaining behind. 37th Divnl. R.A. less Echelon B of the column left for VIth Corps 3rd Army together with Hdqrs Coy of the Train. V.O's sent ½ are Capt. WADDELL, CAPT STANFORD & Lt. JEWELL. Secured motor car & took Lt. YATES to No 4 Coy. 37th Divnl Train. A.S.C.	A.A.P.
"	18.8.16		Morning office & inspected 50th Field Ambulance. Afternoon conference of V.O's & preparing weekly returns. Evening office.	A.A.P.
"	19.8.16		Morning office. Despatched weekly returns. Afternoon visiting sick at DHQ.	A.A.P.
"	20.8.16		Morning office & inspected D.H.Q. horses. Afternoon at Mobile Section. Evening inspected remounts for A.A. & Q.M.G. visited Q office & attended to correspondence.	A.A.P. A.A.P.
"	21.8.16		Morning office & inspected 37th Divnl Signal Coy. R.E. Afternoon at Mobile Section. Evening - office.	
"	22.8.16		Morning office & was informed that 102nd & 103rd Inf. Bdes. were leaving to rejoin 34th Divn. whilst the original 37th Divnl Infantry viz 111th & 112th Bdes. were coming back. No fresh Veterinary arrangements will be necessitated. Thence to DIVION to see 2 horses of M.M.P. suspected of mange & on to PERNES to give opinion on injured civilian horse. Afternoon at M.V.S. Evening office.	A.A.P.

1875 Wt. W593/826 1,000,000 4/15 J.B.C. & A. A.D.S.S./Forms/C. 2118.

Instructions regarding War Diaries and Intelligence Summaries are contained in F. S. Regs., Part II. and the Staff Manual respectively. Title Pages will be prepared in manuscript.

WAR DIARY
or
INTELLIGENCE SUMMARY
(Erase heading not required.)

Army Form C. 2118

Place	Date	Hour	Summary of Events and Information	Remarks and references to Appendices
BRUAY	23.8.16		Morning office & at M.V.S. Afternoon to HERMIN to give instructions to Capt. HUSTON as to taking charge of certain units. Evening office	A.A.P.
"	24.8.16		To railhead at 8 a.m to inspect & distribute 34 remounts. Morning office & visited Signal Coy. At M.V.S. for remainder of the day. 112th Inf. Bde Group proceeded to 40th Divl. Area this day. Lt. J H YATES (T.C) sent in veterinary charge of them	A.A.P.
"	25.8.16		Morning inspected portion of 111th Inf. Bde. Condition good with exception of half a dozen thin animals. Shoeing requires closer attention. Afternoon weekly conference of V.O's & preparing weekly returns for 1st Army	A.A.P.
"	26.8.16		Morning M.V.S. & inspected remainder of 111th Inf. Bde. Heavy rain. Afternoon office & at M.V.S.	A.A.P.
"	27.8.16		Morning at M.V.S. & office. Inspected 50th Field Amb. & 37th Div. Signal Company. Afternoon at M.V.S. Received intimation that Major J.R. STEEVENSON. A.V.C. was being appointed A.D.V.S. 37th Div. Major J.R STEEVENSON arrived 10 p.m	
"	28.8.16		Office at 9 a.m. & handed over A.D.V.S. duties to Major J.R. STEEVENSON.	A.A.P.
			Took over duties of A.D.V.S from Capt. A. A. Pryor. Visited 28 M.V.S in the afternoon	[illegible]
"	29.8.16		Accompanied G.C Divisional Train to inspect 1st Line Transport of 63rd Infantry Brigade	[illegible]
	30.8.16		Office at 9.0 a.m. Inspected Divisional Sig: Coy. Animals in afternoon	[illegible]
	31.8.16		Office at 9.0 a.m. Visited 28 M.V.S. Visited Echelon B. D.A.C in afternoon.	[illegible]

J Steevenson Major
A.D.V.S 37 Division

1875 Wt. W593/826 1,000,000 4/15 J.B.C. & A. A.D.S.S./Forms/C. 2118.

Vol 14

WAR DIARY

Sept 1916

A.D.V.S 37th Divn

Instructions regarding War Diaries and Intelligence Summaries are contained in F. S. Regs., Part II. and the Staff Manual respectively. Title Pages will be prepared in manuscript.

WAR DIARY or INTELLIGENCE SUMMARY

(Erase heading not required.)

A.D.V.S. 37th Division.

Army Form C. 2118

Place	Date	Hour	Summary of Events and Information	Remarks and references to Appendices
BRUAY	1.9/16		Office Visited 37th Div: Signal Coy	[initials]
"	2 9/16		Office. D.D.V.S. 1st Army called at office 10.0 a.m.	[initials]
			(112th Bde (Infty) & 63rd Infty Bde joined division.	[initials]
"	3 9/16		Office – morning. Went to conference of A.D.V.S. at office of D.D.V.S. 1st Army at LILLERS	
"	4 9/16		Office at 9.0 a.m. Visited 50th & 49th Field Ambulances.	[initials]
			Afternoon Visited Nos 2 & 4 Coys 37th Divisional Train	[initials]
"	5 9/16		Office Visited 23. M.V.S.	
"	6 9/16		Office. Visited Divisional Sig: Coy: 1.2 & 3 Section D.A.C & Div: Artillery	[initials]
"	7 9/16		Office at 9.0 a.m. Visited Lt. Yates at 4 Coy Div. Train	[initials]
"	8 9/16		Office. Saw H.Q. changes & Sig: Co.	
"	9 9/16		Office. Weekly returns to D.D.V.S & H.Q. Visited 8th Lincolns transport & Fusiliers	[initials]
"	10 9/16		Office. Visited 9th N. Staffords Transport at Divion	[initials]
"	11 9/16		Office. Visited 23 M.V.S. & 37 Div. Sig: Co.	[initials]
"	12 9/16		Inspected transport animals of whole of 112. Infty: Bde. Office.	[initials]

1875 Wt. W593/826 1,000,000 4/15 J.B.C. & A. A.D.S.S./Forms/C. 2118.

Army Form C. 2118

Instructions regarding War Diaries and Intelligence Summaries are contained in F. S. Regs., Part II. and the Staff Manual respectively. Title Pages will be prepared in manuscript.

WAR DIARY
or
INTELLIGENCE SUMMARY
(Erase heading not required.)

Place	Date	Hour	Summary of Events and Information	Remarks and references to Appendices
BRUAY	13 9/16		Office. Visited 37 Div. Sig: Co: H.Q. chargers & 28 M.V.S. In afternoon went to Beaumetz-les-Aire to collect 4 stray horses under instructions of D.D.V.S. 1st Army. On arrival found that they had already been collected on 8th Sept.	
"	14 9/16		Office. Visited 28 M.V.S.	
"	15 9/16		Office. " 37 Div. R A H Q.	
"	16 9/16		Office. Visited 28 M.V.S.	
"	17 9/16		Office. Visited 37 Div: Artillery at LA THIEULOYE & MAGNICOURT	
"	18 9/16		Office. To BARLIN & arranged about taking over from A.D.V.S. 63rd (RN) Division	
BARLIN	19 9/16		Moved to BARLIN	
	20 9/16		Office. Interviewed V.O's with regard to redistribution of duties. 28 M.V.S arrived from BRUAY & took over billets from 53rd M.V.S. (63rd (R.N) Division)	
"	21 9/16		Office. Visited waggon lines of 123 & 126 Bde R.F.A. at HERSIN & M.M.P. at COUPIGNY.	
"	22 9/16		Office. Visited Echelon B. D.A.C. & No 4 Coy D Train. Saw A.V.C. officers of 37th Division in afternoon.	

1875 Wt. W593/826 1,000,000 4/15 J.B.C. & A. A.D.S.S./Forms/C. 2118.

Instructions regarding War Diaries and Intelligence Summaries are contained in F. S. Regs., Part II. and the Staff Manual respectively. Title Pages will be prepared in manuscript.

WAR DIARY
or
INTELLIGENCE SUMMARY

(Erase heading not required.)

Army Form C. 2118

Place	Date	Hour	Summary of Events and Information	Remarks and references to Appendices
BARLIN	23 9/16		Office. Compiled weekly return. Visited C/123, A/123 Bde R.F.A.	JS
"	24 9/16		Office. Visited A/124, B/124, C/124 & D/124 Bde R.F.A. Handed over No 2 & 3 Sections No 2 Res Park to V.O. i/c IV Corps Cavalry	JS
"	25 9/16		Office. Visited 39 Div Sig: Co. & 28th M.V.S.	JS
"	26 9/16		Office. Visited D/126, B/126, B/124 Batteries 10th Y & L, 49th Field Ambulance & M.M.P. Horses.	JS
"	27 9/16		Office. Visited 28 M.V.S. 39 Sig: Coy ~~Horses~~ & D.H.Q. Horses. 6th Bedfords Transport & 11th Entrenching Batt. Transport	JS
"	28 9/16		Visited transport animals of 63rd, 111th & 112th M. G Coys. & 9th N. Staffords	JS
"	29 9/16		Office. Saw V.O. i/c Bdes & compiling weekly return	JS
"	30 9/16		Office. Visited Transport animals of 112th Infty Bde	JS

J. Stevenson
Major
ADVS 37 Division

1875 Wt. W593/826 1,000,000 4/15 J.B.C. & A. A.D.S.S./Forms/C. 2118.

Instructions regarding War Diaries and Intelligence Summaries are contained in F. S. Regs., Part II. and the Staff Manual respectively. Title Pages will be prepared in manuscript.

WAR DIARY
or
INTELLIGENCE SUMMARY
(Erase heading not required.)

Army Form C. 2118

VOL 15

Place	Date	Hour	Summary of Events and Information	Remarks and references to Appendices
BARLIN	1 10/16		Office. Inspected Horses of B/123 + D/123 R.F.A.	D.
	2 10/16		Office. Inspected horses of C/123 + A/123 R.F.A. Condemned two horses to be evacuated for debility from C/123 & one horse for debility from A/123	D.
	3 10/16		Office. Saw D. Commander about number of destructions in division in past week.	D.
	4 10/16		Visited B/124 R.F.A. 5 horses of this unit for evacuation for debility. Also visited transport 4th Middlesex. Several cases of colic in D.A.C. & 124/Bde R.F.A. caused by the red clay put down for horse standings. Advised that chalk be mixed with it to ~~[illegible]~~ cause it to bind.	D.
	5 10/16		Office. Visited A/126, B/126, & D/124 Battery R.F.A. Saw that attention was being paid to horse standings.	D.
	6 10/16		Compiling weekly returns. Conference of V.Os of division in afternoon.	D.
	7 10/16		Office. Forwarded A.F. 2000 for week ending 5/10/16. Visited C/123 RFA with C.R.A.	
	8 10/16		Attended conference at D.D.V.S. 1st Army. LILLERS	D.
	9 10/16		Office. C/126 Battery arrived from England with 178 animals	D.
	10 10/16		Visited C/124 & C/126 Batteries. In afternoon to C/126 R.F.A. Evacuated 3 horses for debility.	D.

1875 Wt. W593/826 1,000,000 4/15 J.B.C. & A. A.D.S.S./Forms/C. 2118.

Instructions regarding War Diaries and Intelligence Summaries are contained in F. S. Regs., Part II. and the Staff Manual respectively. Title Pages will be prepared in manuscript.

WAR DIARY
or
INTELLIGENCE SUMMARY
(Erase heading not required.)

Army Form C. 2118

Place	Date	Hour	Summary of Events and Information	Remarks and references to Appendices
BARLIN	11/10/16		Visited No 1 Sec: D.A.C. & arranged to evacuate 5 mules & 22 horses from animals joining D.A.C. from C/26 Battery for debility. Afternoon inspected 9th N. Staffords & 48th Field Ambulance Transport with O.C. 37 Div: Train	
"	12/10/16		Office. Visited C/26 R.F.A. & saw horses tested with Mallein. No reactions. Afternoon inspection of 37th Div: Train with O.C. CAPTAIN J.A STANFORD A.V.C. left for duty at No 4 BASE REMOUNT DEPOT. BOULOGNE.	
"	13/10/16		Office. Compiling A.F 2000. Conference of V. Os.	
	14/10/16		Captain S. F SPURR A V C (T.C) joined for duty from Indian Vety Hospital ROUEN. Completed A.F 2000 & despatched same.	
	15/10/16		Distributed 122 remounts at BARLIN station. D.D.V.S & D.D of Remounts visited No 28. M.V.S.	
	16/10/16		Office. Inspected horses in M.V.S prior to evacuation	
	17/10/16		As usual	
	18/10/16		Marched from Barlin to ROELLECOURT. M.V.S marched with Divisional artillery.	

1875 Wt. W593/826 1,000,000 4/15 J.B.C. & A. A.D.S.S./Forms/C. 2118.

Instructions regarding War Diaries and Intelligence Summaries are contained in F. S. Regs., Part II. and the Staff Manual respectively. Title pages will be prepared in manuscript.

WAR DIARY
or
INTELLIGENCE SUMMARY.
(Erase heading not required.)

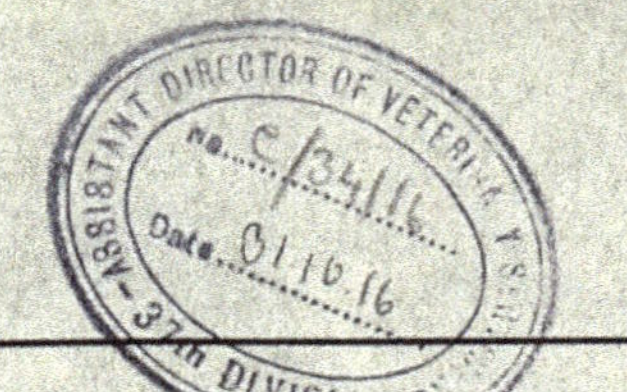

Army Form C. 2118.

Place	Date	Hour	Summary of Events and Information	Remarks and references to Appendices
ROELLECOURT	19/10/16		Halted all day	JB
"	20/10/16		Marched from ROELLECOURT to LECAUROY.	JB
LE CAUROY	21/10/16		LE CAUROY to BEAUVAL by road	JB
MARIEUX	22/10/16		BEAUVAL to MARIEUX. Saw DDVS Reserve Army & reported	JB
"	23/10/16		M.V.S arrived at ORVILLE with Divisional Artillery	JB
"	24/10/16		Arranged for billets of M.V.S at ORVILLE with Town Major. Divisional Artillery left Division to be attached to other divisions for a time.	JB
"	25/10/16		M.V.S from ORVILLE to MARIEUX as the accommodation at former place is wanted for other troops. Arranged for M.V.S to be at D.H.Q. as less likely to be moved about by other troops coming in.	JB

A5834 Wt. W4973/M687 750,000 8/16 D. D. & L. Ltd. Forms/C.2118/13

Instructions regarding War Diaries and Intelligence Summaries are contained in F. S. Regs., Part II. and the Staff Manual respectively. Title pages will be prepared in manuscript.

WAR DIARY
or
INTELLIGENCE SUMMARY.
(Erase heading not required.)

Army Form C. 2118.

Place	Date	Hour	Summary of Events and Information	Remarks and references to Appendices
MARIEUX	26/10/16		Interviewed D.D.V.S. Reserve Army & after to railhead at BELLE EGLISE to arrange evacuation of horses from M.V.S. Visited 124th R.F.A. wagon lines at VARENNES & No 3 Coy Divisional Train	
"	27/10/16		Conference of Vety Officers Compiling A.F.A 2000.	
"	28/10/16		Visited detachments of artillery brigades & D.A.C at AMPLIER Arranged for collection of 4 horses at AMPLIER left behind by 8th Divisional artillery.	
"	29/10/16		Inspected 123 Bde R.F.A at HEDAUVILLE Inspected sick horses in M.V.S prior to evacuation. Inspected some horses of 126 Bde RFA at ACHEUX.	
"	30/10/16		Visited R.F.A Bde details & D.A.C at AMPLIER. Made suggestions to D.A.D.O.S. re improvised pack saddle for 18 pr: ammunition	
"	31/10/16		Correspondence. Saw pack saddle fitted & suggested alterations in same. One H.D. mare belonging to Divisional H.Q. died from twisted intestine: To M.V.S. & saw horses to be evacuated.	

J. Stevenson Major
ADVS 37 Division

A5834 Wt. W4973/M687 750,000 8/16 D. D. & L. Ltd. Forms/C.2118/13

Instructions regarding War Diaries and Intelligence Summaries are contained in F. S. Regs., Part II. and the Staff Manual respectively. Title pages will be prepared in manuscript.

WAR DIARY
or
INTELLIGENCE SUMMARY.
(Erase heading not required.)

Army Form C. 2118.

ADVS 37 D Vol 16

Place	Date	Hour	Summary of Events and Information	Remarks and references to Appendices
MARIEUX	1.11/16		To AMPLIER & arranged collection of 1 LD Horse & 1 mule left behind by 21st D.A.C. These two animals were fit for work & were absorbed into 37th D.A.C. Afterwards to HEM to collect 1 horse but found horse had already been collected by 22 M.V.S	[initials]
"	2 11/16		With O.C Train to BEAUVAL to inspect pack saddles & improvised pack saddles of 63rd Infty Bde. The latter unsuitable. Afternoon to 112th Infty Bde at GEZAINCOURT to see pack saddlery, & then to see same of 9th N Staffords Pioneers at BEAUVAL	[initials]
"	3 11/16		Office. To M.V.S to see animals for evacuation. Afternoon conference of V. Offr units	[initials]
"	4 11/16		To 124th Bde R.F.A at Varennes. Compiling weekly returns	[initials]
"	5 11/16		Office. To M.V.S to see horses for evacuation.	[initials]
"	6 11/16		To D.A.C + detachments R.F.A Brigades at GRVILLE-AMPLIER arranged collection of 3 horses from GRVILLE left behind by 56th Div Artillery	[initials]
"	7 11/16		Office. To 28 M.V.S to see horses for evacuation.	[initials]

A5834 Wt. W4973/M687 750,000 8/16 D. D. & L. Ltd. Forms/C.2118/13

WAR DIARY
or
INTELLIGENCE SUMMARY.
(Erase heading not required.)

Army Form C. 2118.

Place	Date	Hour	Summary of Events and Information	Remarks and references to Appendices
MARIEUX	8 11/16		To HEM to collect Horse of 21st DAC. Found animal incurably injured & destroyed the same	JS.
"	9 11/16		Office. To 28 M.V.S to see horses for evacuation. D.D.V.S. Fifth Army inspected the 28 M.V.S in afternoon	JS.
"	10 11/16		To inspect horses of C/126 & B/126/RFA at ACHEUX & then to HEDAUVILLE to see No 1 Sec: D.A.C. Afternoon conference of V.O's &	JS.
"	11 11/16		Compiling A.FA.2000 & weekly returns.	JS.
"	12 11/16		Inspected 123/Bde R.F.A. & selected 8 horses for evacuation for debility. To M.V.S to see horses for evacuation.	JS.
"	13 11/16		Office & to 28 M.V.S. to see horses for evacuation	JS.
"	14 11/16		Instructed M.V.S. to evacuate all horses under treatment & prepare to move on 16.11.16. Office.	JS.

A5834 Wt. W4973/M687 750,000 8/16 D. D. & L. Ltd. Forms/C.2118/13.

Instructions regarding War Diaries and Intelligence Summaries are contained in F. S. Regs., Part II. and the Staff Manual respectively. Title pages will be prepared in manuscript.

WAR DIARY
or
INTELLIGENCE SUMMARY.
(Erase heading not required.)

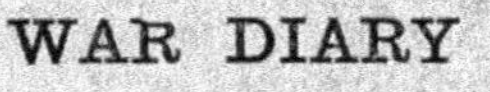

Army Form C. 2118.

Place	Date	Hour	Summary of Events and Information	Remarks and references to Appendices
MARIEUX	15/11/16		To GRVILLE to see animals of D.A.C. & R.F.A. details	[initials]
HEDAUVILLE	16.11.16		Moved D.H.Q. to HEDAUVILLE	[initials]
FORCEVILLE			Moved to FORCEVILLE. Inspected pack transport at MESNIL & afterwards to see animals of 112th Infty Bde. Conference of V.O.s in afternoon	[initials]
"	18/11/16		Compiling weekly returns	[initials]
"	19/11/16		To M.V.S. to see animals left behind by 53rd M.V.S. about 100. 75 evacuated & 15 float cases left over until later. To Acheux to arrange about trucks for the 15 float cases on 20/11/16. Afterwards to Advanced D.H.Q. to see animals of Sig. Coy & 49 Field Ambulance	[initials]
"	20/11/16		To M.V.S. to see animals. Afterwards to Advanced D.H.Q.	[initials]
"	21/11/16		To Advanced D.H.Q. in morning & in afternoon to GRVILLE to see H.Q. 37 D.A.C. & details R.F.A. Bdes.	[initials]
"	22/11/16		To 126/Bde R.F.A. at ACHEUX. Noted 8 horses for evacuation for debility & cracked heels. In afternoon saw two horses affected with mange belonging to a French civilian at FORCEVILLE. Notified A.P.M. D.D.V.S. & Town Major	[initials]

A5834 Wt. W4973/M687 750,000 8/16 D. D. & L. Ltd. Forms/C.2118/13

Instructions regarding War Diaries and Intelligence Summaries are contained in F. S. Regs., Part II. and the Staff Manual respectively. Title pages will be prepared in manuscript.

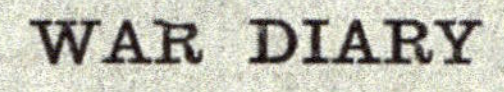

WAR DIARY
or
INTELLIGENCE SUMMARY.
(Erase heading not required.)

Army Form C. 2118.

Place	Date	Hour	Summary of Events and Information	Remarks and references to Appendices
FORCEVILLE	23/11/16		To Advanced D.H.Q. & to see horses of 8 Cavalry Pioneer Battn & Transport of 63rd Infty Brigade	[illegible]
"	24/11/16		To Advanced D.H.Q. & in afternoon conference of V.O.s. Capt. A.A. Pryce AVC O.C. 28 M.V.S. went on leave to England. Capt. Yates AVC [illegible] in temporary command of 28 M.V.S. during Capt. Pryce's absence	[illegible]
MARIEUX	25/11/16		Hd Qrs & 28 M.V.S. moved to MARIEUX. Disinfection weekly state to D.D.V.S. Fifth Army	[illegible]
"	26/11/16		26 horses collected from [illegible] by motor ambulance & taken to 28 M.V.S.	[illegible]
"	27/11/16		Saw D.D.V.S. at MARIEUX re [illegible] two horses of 8 Bde 32nd Canadian Divisional Artillery to 28 M.V.S.	[illegible]
"	28/11/16		To M.V.S. to see [illegible] for evacuation	
"	29/11/16		To BEAUQUESNE to try to find billet for M.V.S. Found nothing suitable	[illegible]
"	30/11/16		To ARQUEVES & BEAUQUESNE. To M.V.S. to see animals.	[illegible]

[illegible signature]
Major AVC
ADVS 37 Division

A5834 Wt. W4973/M687 750,000 8/16 D. D. & L. Ltd. Forms/C.2118/13

Instructions regarding War Diaries and Intelligence Summaries are contained in F. S. Regs., Part II. and the Staff Manual respectively. Title pages will be prepared in manuscript.

WAR DIARY
or
INTELLIGENCE SUMMARY.
(*Erase heading not required.*)

Army Form C. 2118.

Vol 17

Place	Date	Hour	Summary of Events and Information	Remarks and references to Appendices
MARIEUX	1 12/16		To VERT-GALAND (about 9 miles from here) to see a horse left behind by B Battery 150 Bde R F A. Found horse incurably lame from [illegible] + affected with mange so destroyed him. Conference of V.O.s in afternoon + to M.V.S. to see horses.	[illegible]
	2 12/16		Compiling returns (weekly states) + despatched same. Reported on the frog protectors to D.D.V.S. (Not [illegible] [illegible] [illegible] [illegible] [illegible]) To M.V.S. to see horses. Expected visit from 11th [illegible] re location of M.V.S. in ARQUEVES but no information received	[illegible]
	3 12/16		To THIEVRES to see 3 horses left behind by units + arranged their collection by No 41 M.V.S. at AUTHIE. To 28 M.V.S. to see animals for [illegible]. To see D.D.V.S. [illegible] [illegible] re [illegible] of horses with the frog protectors.	[illegible]
	4 12/16		No 28 M.V.S. moved to ARQUEVES. [illegible] [illegible] [illegible] of [illegible] with the frog protectors as they are not durable + do not last much more than a day	[illegible]
	5 12/16		To ARQUEVES to No 28 M.V.S. Office	[illegible]
	6 12/16		To 28 M.V.S. Office	[illegible]
	7 12/16		To 28 M.V.S. + afterwards to inspect wagon lines of D/225 + C/126 R F A	[illegible]
	8 12/16		To M.V.S. Saw V.O.s at office in afternoon with weekly states.	[illegible]
	9 12/16		Capt. A. A. Pryer A.V.C. returned from leave. Compiling weekly state for D.D.V.S.	[illegible]

A5834 Wt. W4973/M687 750,000 8/16 D. D. & L. Ltd. Forms/C.2118/13

Instructions regarding War Diaries and Intelligence Summaries are contained in F. S. Regs., Part II. and the Staff Manual respectively. Title pages will be prepared in manuscript.

WAR DIARY
or
INTELLIGENCE SUMMARY.
(Erase heading not required.)

Army Form C. 2118.

Place	Date	Hour	Summary of Events and Information	Remarks and references to Appendices
MARIEUX	10.12.16		Major J R STEEVENSON proceeded on leave to United Kingdom. Capt. A A PRYER took over duties of A D V S. Captain J. H. YATES remains in temporary command of 28th MOBILE VETY SECTION.	AAP
"	11.12.16		Morning inspected D H Q horses & 34th Divl Signal Coy R E. Afternoon office. Received preliminary orders that the Division would concentrate preparatory to moving. Warned O.C. M.V.S and other officers accordingly.	AAP
	12.12.16		Morning office and to 28th M.V.S at ARQUEVES. Afternoon office	AAP
"	13.12.16		Morning to M.V.S at ARQUEVES. Afternoon office. Evening preparing to move next day.	
FROHEN-LE-GRAND	14.12.16		Marched from MARIEUX at 9 a.m. arriving at FROHEN-LE-GRAND at 1 pm	AAP
FLERS	15.12.16		Marched via FORTEL and LIGNY to FLERS	AAP
MONCHY-CAYEUX	16.12.16		Marched from FLERS to MONCHY-CAYEUX via St. POL. Arrived noon	AAP
NORRENTES-FONTES	17.12.16		Marched from MONCHY-CAYEUX to NORRENTES FONTES via BERGENEUSE and WESTERHAM. Arrived noon.	AAP
St VENANT	18.12.16		Marched from NORRENTES FONTES at 9 a.m. to St VENANT via LILLERS arriving at 11 a.m.	AAP
"	19.12.16		Spent day in visiting new Divisional Area & searching for suitable billets for waggon lines & M.V.S. No great success. Horse standings are scanty.	AAP
"	20.12.16		Again visited new Area. Selected spot for M.V.S. Open standings & no cover but centrally situated & near water & railhead.	AAP
"	21.12.16		Morning inspected D.H.Q. horses & Signal Company & prepared to move. Left at 1.30 p.m	
LESTREM			arriving LESTREM at 3 pm. M.V.S situated on outskirts of village at R 8 d 9 0 (Combined BETHUNE map).	AAP

A5834 Wt. W4973/M687 750,000 8/16 D. D. & L. Ltd. Forms/C.2118/13

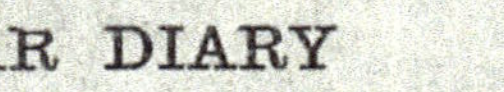

Instructions regarding War Diaries and Intelligence Summaries are contained in F. S. Regs., Part II. and the Staff Manual respectively. Title pages will be prepared in manuscript.

WAR DIARY
or
INTELLIGENCE SUMMARY.
(Erase heading not required.)

Army Form C. 2118.

Place	Date	Hour	Summary of Events and Information	Remarks and references to Appendices
LESTREM	22.12.16		Morning office & to M.V.S.	
"	23 12/16		MAJOR J R STEEVENSON returned from leave to England & took over duties of ADVS from Capt: A A Pryer.	
"	24 12/16		Morning Office & afternoon to select site for 28 M.V.S at FOSSE	
"	25 12/16		Inspected 48th Field Ambulance & afterwards to 63rd Infy Bde H.Q. & then to see transport animals of 8th Lincolns, & to 28th M.V.S. Received wire saying D.D.V.S 1st Army would call at office on 26.12.16	
"	26 12/16		Office. D.D.V.S. 1st Army called in afternoon & afterwards went to see site for 28 M.V.S of which he approved.	
	27 12/16		To ST. VENANT & inspected 123 & 126 Btts R.F.A.	
	28 12/16		Inspected 112th M.G. Coy: 49th & 50th Field Ambulances & then saw horses of M.V.S prior to their evacuation.	
	29 12/16		To M.V.S & in afternoon conference of V.O.s & compiling weekly states	
	30 12/16		To M.V.S & afternoon to H.Q. Coy & No 3 Coy Divisional Train. Dispatched weekly states	
	31 12/16		Office & to M.V.S in afternoon	

A5834 Wt. W4973/M687 750,000 8/16 D. D. & L. Ltd. Forms/C.2118/13

Army Form C. 2118.

Instructions regarding War Diaries and Intelligence Summaries are contained in F. S. Regs., Part II. and the Staff Manual respectively. Title Pages will be prepared in manuscript.

WAR DIARY
or
INTELLIGENCE SUMMARY

(Erase heading not required.)

ADVS 37 D

Vol 18

Place	Date	Hour	Summary of Events and Information	Remarks and references to Appendices
LESTREM	1.1/17		To M.V.S + 1st Pontoon Park R.E. Office. Wire received for Capt. A.A. Pryer AVC to report to H.Q. D.V.S. for duty forthwith. Lt. R.S.L. BEAUMONT A.V.C (T.F) being sent in relief	
"	2 1/17		Inspected transport animals of 112 Bde. Visited 1st Pontoon Park R.E.	
"	3 1/17		Noticed D.D.V.S 1st Army that 26 animals 37 Div were evacuated by 28 M.V.S today. CAPTAIN A.A. PRYER AVC left for H.Q. D.V.S. Captain Yates took over 28 M.V.S. Inspected 104 R.A. remounts at LA GORGUE Station. In afternoon inspected C/124 R.F.A at PARADIS. Accompanied D.D.R to inspect 4 animals for evacuation for Remount Reasons	
"	4 1/17		Inspected A/124 B/124 + C/124 R.F.A. Also 136 Heavy Battery. 3 cases of mange in latter + ordered evacuation of same + all precautions as to isolation disinfection etc to be taken. In afternoon inspected No 1 Sec. 37 D.A.C. Selected 15 horses for evacuation for debility. Lieut R.S.L BEAUMONT A.V.C reported for duty + posted to 126/Bde R.F.A.	
"	5 1/17		To M.V.S. Conference of V.O's in afternoon. 34 animals evacuated by M.V.S	
"	6 1/17		Inspected No 2 Section D.A.C + selected 8 horses for evacuation for debility. Afterwards visited No 3 Section D.A.C. Compiled weekly return + despatched same to D.D.V.S 1st Army	
"	7 1/17		To M.V.S + inspected sick horses + afterwards to D/126 R.F.A	
"	8 1/17		Inspected transport animals of Somerset L. Infty + then to M.V.S Office	

2449 Wt. W14957/M90 750,000 1/16 J.B.C. & A. Forms/C.2118/12.

Instructions regarding War Diaries and Intelligence Summaries are contained in F. S. Regs., Part II. and the Staff Manual respectively. Title pages will be prepared in manuscript.

WAR DIARY
or
INTELLIGENCE SUMMARY.
(Erase heading not required.)

Army Form C. 2118.

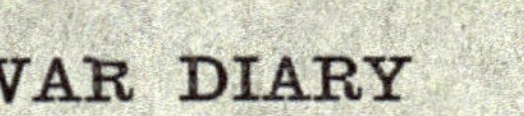

Place	Date	Hour	Summary of Events and Information	Remarks and references to Appendices
LESTREM	9/1/17		Inspected No 3 Sec D.A.C. Selected 10 horses for evacuation for debility. To M.V.S. Uprights received by Pat[illegible] for horse standings	[illegible]
"	10/1/17		Office & to M.V.S.	[illegible]
"	11/1/17		To M.V.S. & office	[illegible]
"	12/1/17		Conference of V.O's & compiling weekly states. Capt J. Waddell AVC returned from leave to England	[illegible]
"	13/1/17		Capt. W. Huston A.V.C. left on leave to England. Gave a lecture at Artillery School LOCON. Despatched weekly states to D.D.V.S. 1st Army	[illegible]
"	14/1/17		Attended a conference of A.D.s V.S. at office of D.D.V.S. 1st Army LILLERS. Office work & visit to M.V.S. Reported to D.D.V.S. re methods of protective shoeing for picking up nails	[illegible]
"	15/1/17		Visited all the Sections of D.A.C. with Staff Captain R.A. In afternoon to M.V.S. & office	[illegible]
"	16/1/17		Accompanied XI Corps Commander & Divisional Commander round horse lines of Division	[illegible]

A5834 Wt. W4973/M687 750,000 8/16 D. D. & L. Ltd. Forms/C.2118/13

Instructions regarding War Diaries and Intelligence Summaries are contained in F. S. Regs., Part II. and the Staff Manual respectively. Title pages will be prepared in manuscript.

WAR DIARY
or
INTELLIGENCE SUMMARY.
(Erase heading not required.)

Army Form C. 2118.

Place	Date	Hour	Summary of Events and Information	Remarks and references to Appendices
LESTREM	17/1/17		Visited M.V.S & also 48th Field Ambulance. Office.	JS
"	18/1/17		Inspected horses in M.V.S & also C/126 Bde & A/123 Bde R F A Office.	JS
"	19/1/17		To M.V.S. Conference of V. O's of Division	JS
"	20/1/17		Compiled & despatched weekly states to D.D.V.S. Met D.D.R 1st Army at M.V.S to cast some animals	JS
"	21/1/17		Inspected transport animals of 4th Middlesex Regt. & 8th Lincolns. To M.V.S & office	JS
"	22/1/17		Inspected transport animals of 11th Warwicks & 13th R Fusiliers. Visited C/126 R.F.A & M.V.S. Reported that Sergts are attached D/126 & No 3 Sec: D.A.C would become surplus in reorganisation of artillery of Division.	JS JS
"	23/1/17		Visited M.V.S. Office. Inspected 131 Remounts that arrived for division at LA GORGUE station.	JS
"	24/1/17		To M.V.S & office.	JS

A5834 Wt. W4973/M687 750,000 8/16 D. D. & L. Ltd. Forms/C.2118/13

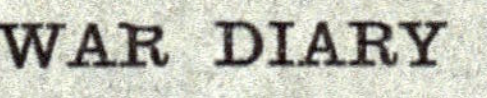

Instructions regarding War Diaries and Intelligence Summaries are contained in F. S. Regs., Part II. and the Staff Manual respectively. Title pages will be prepared in manuscript.

WAR DIARY
or
INTELLIGENCE SUMMARY.
(Erase heading not required.)

Army Form C. 2118.

Place	Date	Hour	Summary of Events and Information	Remarks and references to Appendices
LESTREM.	25th/1		To M.V.S. & to C/124 R.F.A. & office to 37 D.A.C.	[initials]
	26th/1		Conference of V.O.S. To M.V.S. & inspected horses before evacuation. Fitted with Anti gas box respirator	[initials]
"	27th/1		Visited M.V.S. Despatched weekly states to D.D.V.S. 1st Army. Office	[initials]
	28th/1		Visited M.V.S. Office	
	29th/1		Accompanied D.D.V.S. 1st Army & B.G. R.A. to all the R.A. units of the division	[initials]
	30th/1		Inspected transport animals of 111th Infy Bde. Office	[initials]
"	31st/1		To M.V.S. Office. Received report of D.D.V.S. on his inspection of R.A. units on 29th/1. Report states that condition of animals is very satisfactory	[initials]

[signature]
Major
ADVS 37 Divn

A5834 Wt. W4973/M687 750,000 8/16 D. D. & L. Ltd. Forms/C.2118/13

WAR DIARY. Vol 19

A.D.V.S. 37th DIVN. Feb 1917

Instructions regarding War Diaries and Intelligence Summaries are contained in F. S. Regs., Part II. and the Staff Manual respectively. Title pages will be prepared in manuscript.

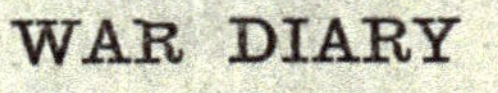

WAR DIARY
or
INTELLIGENCE SUMMARY.
(Erase heading not required.)

Army Form C. 2118.

Place	Date	Hour	Summary of Events and Information	Remarks and references to Appendices
LESTREM	1/2/17		To M.V.S. Office	
"	2/2/17		To M.V.S. Office. Conference of V.O's of Division. Preparing weekly states.	
"	3/2/17		Inspected animals of C/124 + D/123 R F A + H Q Coy Div. Train. Sent weekly states to D.D.V.S. First Army + D.H.Q	
"	4/2/17		To Fellers to attend conference of A.D's V.S. with D.D.V.S. 1st Army. In afternoon with Divisional Commander to inspect A/123 + B/123/RFA	
"	5/2/17		To H Q Coy Div. Train to inspect horses, afterwards to C/124 + D/123 RFA. To M.V.S. + Office	
"	6/2/17		With Divisional Commander to inspect 37th D.A.C + in afternoon to inspect 9th N. Staffords.	
"	7/2/17		With Divisional Commander to inspect 50 + 48 Field Ambulances + 152 + 153 Field Coys R.E. In afternoon to 49 Field Ambulance	
"	8/2/17		With Divisional Commander to inspect 13th K.R.R.C + 13th Rifle Brigade + 111th Machine Gun Coy: + in afternoon Divisional H Q + Divisional Signal Coy R E	

A5834 Wt. W4973/M687 750,000 8/16 D. D. & L. Ltd. Forms/C.2118/13

Instructions regarding War Diaries and Intelligence Summaries are contained in F. S. Regs., Part II. and the Staff Manual respectively. Title pages will be prepared in manuscript.

WAR DIARY
or
INTELLIGENCE SUMMARY.
(Erase heading not required.)

Army Form C. 2118.

Place	Date	Hour	Summary of Events and Information	Remarks and references to Appendices
LESTREM	9/2/17		Conference of V.Os of Division. Preparing weekly returns	[illegible]
	10/2/17		Went to NOEUX-LES-MINES to arrange with ADVS 24th Division about taking over from him on 13th inst	[illegible]
	11/2/17		To MVS & then to 1?01 Sec. DAC & B/123 R.F.A.	[illegible]
	12/2/17		Closed down MVS preparatory to marching tomorrow	[illegible]
	13/2/17		Marched to BRACQUEMONT (NOEUX-LES-MINES)	[illegible]
BRACQUEMONT	14/2/17		Visited M.VS at DROUVIN & inspected 22 Remounts on arrival at station	[illegible]
	15/2/17		Visited A/108 & B/108 Army F.A. & 37th Sig. Coy. In afternoon to attend a lecture by Lt. Col. Wash A.A. Q.M.G. 6th Division on Administrative Arrangements made by a Division during the offensive on the Somme. Lecture was held at LILLERS	[illegible]
	16/2/17		Conference of V.O.S. Visited M.V.S. Compiling weekly returns	[illegible]
	17/2/17		Inspected 170 & 173 Tunnelling Coys & 49 Field Ambulance. [signature]	[illegible]

A5834 Wt. W4973/M687 750,000 8/16 D. D. & L. Ltd. Forms/C.2118/13

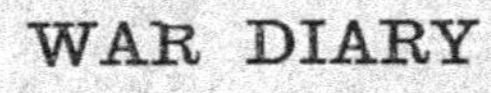

WAR DIARY
or
INTELLIGENCE SUMMARY.
(Erase heading not required.)

Instructions regarding War Diaries and Intelligence Summaries are contained in F. S. Regs., Part II. and the Staff Manual respectively. Title pages will be prepared in manuscript.

Army Form C. 2118.

Place	Date	Hour	Summary of Events and Information	Remarks and references to Appendices
BRAQUEMONT	18 2/17		Inspected ^transport of^ 8th Lincolns 63rd M.G. Coy. 152 Coy RE & 10th R Fusiliers Visited 28 M.V.S. at DROUVIN. Inspected No 3 Sec. G[?] Res Park.	
"	19 2/17		To M.V.S. & Office. Inspected 112th Infty Bde Transport.	
"	20 2/17		Accompanied Divisional Commander round all the Infty Transport & M.G. Coys of the Division. In afternoon attended a lecture by Maj: Gen Ford on 'Administrative Arrangements made by a Corps during the offensive on the Somme'	
"	21 2/17		Inspected 123 Bde R.F.A. In afternoon with Divisional Commander to inspect 37th D.A.C	
"	22 2/17		To M.V.S. & H.Q. Coy 37th Divl Train. In afternoon to attend a lecture by Brig: Gen: May D.S.O. D.A. & Q.M.G. 2nd Corps on Administrative Arrangements made by an Army during the offensive on the Somme	
	23 2/17		Inspected A B C /124 Bde. Conference of V.Os in afternoon & preparing weekly states	
	24 2/17		Inspected D/124/R.F.A. Office. Despatched weekly states.	

A5834 Wt. W4973/M687 750,000 8/16 D. D. & L. Ltd. Forms/C.2118/13

Instructions regarding War Diaries and Intelligence Summaries are contained in F. S. Regs., Part II. and the Staff Manual respectively. Title pages will be prepared in manuscript.

WAR DIARY
or
INTELLIGENCE SUMMARY.
(Erase heading not required.)

Army Form C. 2118.

Place	Date	Hour	Summary of Events and Information	Remarks and references to Appendices
BRAQUEMONT	25 2/17		To M.V.S. Office.	
"	26 2/17		Visited 123/Bde R.F.A. Office. A.D.V.S. 6th Division called at office	
"	27 2/17		To M.V.S. + then to No 2 Sec: D.A.C. Inspected H.Q. Coy Divisional Train	
"	28 2/17		Office.	

J. [illegible] Major
A.D.V.S. 37th Division

A5834 Wt. W4973/M687 750,000 8/16 D. D. & L. Ltd. Forms/C.2118/13

MARCH 1917

Vol 20

WAR DIARY

A.D.V.S. 37th DIVN

Instructions regarding War Diaries and Intelligence Summaries are contained in F. S. Regs., Part II. and the Staff Manual respectively. Title pages will be prepared in manuscript.

WAR DIARY
or
INTELLIGENCE SUMMARY.
(Erase heading not required.)

Army Form C. 2118.

Place	Date	Hour	Summary of Events and Information	Remarks and references to Appendices
BRAQUEMONT	1 3/17		To 28 M.V.S. CAPTAIN J. WADDELL. A.V.C. left for duty at No 22 Vety: Hospital. ABBEVILLE	[illegible]
"	2 3/17		Compiling weekly states. Conference of V.O's. in afternoon	[illegible]
"	3 3/17		Despatched weekly states. Office	
NORRENT-FONTES.	4 3/17		Marched to NORRENT FONTES 28 M.V.S. moved to same place.	[illegible]
"	5 3/17		Visited 124 Bde R.F.A. at BERGUETTE	[illegible]
"	6 3/17		" 123 Bde RFA at GUARBECQUE.	[illegible]
"	7 3/17		To M.V.S. & Office. Called at office of D.D.V.S. 1st Army at LILLERS.	
"	8 3/17		Compiling weekly states. Visited 123 Bde R.F.A.	[illegible]
"	9 3/17		Moved to ROELLECOURT. M.V.S. moved to ROCOURT ST LAURENT. Reported to D.D.V.S. 3rd Army	

A5834 Wt. W4973/M687 750,000 8/16 D. D. & L. Ltd. Forms/C.2118/13

Instructions regarding War Diaries and Intelligence Summaries are contained in F. S. Regs., Part II. and the Staff Manual respectively. Title pages will be prepared in manuscript.

WAR DIARY
or
INTELLIGENCE SUMMARY.
(Erase heading not required.)

Army Form C. 2118.

Place	Date	Hour	Summary of Events and Information	Remarks and references to Appendices
ROELLECOURT.				
"	10 3/17		Visited 112 Infty Bde.	
"	11 3/17		To M.V.S. & also R.F.A Bdes & D.A.C at ST. MICHEL	
"	12 3/17		To H.Q Coy Train & after to arrange with R.T.O. ST. POL re evacuation of sick animals	
"	13 3/17		To M.V.S & after to 111th Infty Bde	
"	14 3/17		To M.V.S. & after to artillery Bdes.	
"	15 3/17		To 123 & 124 Bde R.F.A. Office	
"	16 3/17		Divisional Artillery left to join VII Corps accompanied by Lieut. S.F. Spurr: A.V.C. & Lieut. Beaumont A.V.C. Echelon B of D.A.C remains with division	
"	17 3/17		To M.V.S & to office of D.D.V.S. 3rd Army	
"	18 3/17		Visited transport lines of 13th K.R.R.C 13th R.B 8th Lincolns & Nos 2 & 3 Coys of Divisional Train	

A5834 Wt. W4973/M687 750,000 8/16 D. D. & L. Ltd. Forms/C.2118/13

Instructions regarding War Diaries and Intelligence Summaries are contained in F. S. Regs., Part II. and the Staff Manual respectively. Title pages will be prepared in manuscript.

Army Form C. 2118.

WAR DIARY
or
INTELLIGENCE SUMMARY.
(Erase heading not required.)

Place	Date	Hour	Summary of Events and Information	Remarks and references to Appendices
ROELLE-COURT	19/3/17		To M V S & B. Echelon 37th D.A.C	[initials]
	20/3/17		Visited 8th Somersets, 111th M.G Coy. 63rd M.G Coy, & 10th R. Fusiliers	[initials]
"	21/3/17		Judged with G.C. Train at a transport competition of 112 Infy Bde. at ESTREE WAMIN. Visited M V S all cases evacuated as Division is under short notice to move	[initials]
	22/3/17		To M.V.S & Office. Also visited transport animals of 13th R.F & 8th Lincolns.	[initials]
"	23/3/17		Compiling of weekly states. Conference of V.O's in afternoon	[initials]
"	24/3/17		Dispatched weekly states & visited M.V.S Office routine	[initials]
"	25/3/17		To M V.S & Office	
"	26/3/17		To M.V.S Two cases of Stomatitis Contagiosa admitted from 17th D A C	[initials]

A5834 Wt. W4973/M687 750,000 8/16 D. D. & L. Ltd. Forms/C.2118/13

Army Form C. 2118.

Instructions regarding War Diaries and Intelligence Summaries are contained in F. S. Regs., Part II. and the Staff Manual respectively. Title pages will be prepared in manuscript.

WAR DIARY
or
INTELLIGENCE SUMMARY.
(Erase heading not required.)

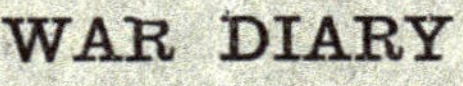

Place	Date	Hour	Summary of Events and Information	Remarks and references to Appendices
ROELLE-COURT.	27/3/17		To M.V.S. Office routine	
"	28.3.17		To 63rd Infty Bde H.Q. & then to 11th R. Warwick to see a case of suspected Mange. Ordered evacuation	J.S.
"	29 3/17		To M.V.S. Office.	J.S.
"	30 3/17		Conference of V.Os. Compiling weekly states. To M.V.S.	J.S.
"	31 3/17		Despatched weekly states. Judged at a transport competition of 63rd Infty Bde	J.S.
			J Stewart Major ADVS 37 Division	J.S.

A5834 Wt. W4973/M687 750,000 8/16 D. D. & L. Ltd. Forms/C.2118/13

War Diary

A.D.V.S. 37th Divn.

Apl 1917

Vol 21

Instructions regarding War Diaries and Intelligence Summaries are contained in F. S. Regs., Part II. and the Staff Manual respectively. Title pages will be prepared in manuscript.

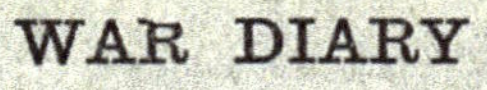

WAR DIARY
or
INTELLIGENCE SUMMARY.
(Erase heading not required.)

Army Form C. 2118.

Place	Date	Hour	Summary of Events and Information	Remarks and references to Appendices
ROELLE-COURT	1/4/17		To M.V.S. & usual routine	JT
	2/4/17		Visited Transport of 63rd Infty Bde.	JT
	3/4/17		Usual routine.	JT
	4/4/17		Usual routine. Major Stevenson ADVS to 12th Stationary Hospital with German Measles. Handed over duties to Capt J. H. Yates AVC & reported same to DDVS 3rd Army	JT

A5834 Wt. W4973/M687 750,000 8/16 D. D. & L. Ltd. Forms/C.2118/13

Instructions regarding War Diaries and Intelligence Summaries are contained in F. S. Regs., Part II. and the Staff Manual respectively. Title pages will be prepared in manuscript.

WAR DIARY
or
INTELLIGENCE SUMMARY.

(Erase heading not required.)

Army Form C. 2118.

Place	Date	Hour	Summary of Events and Information	Remarks and references to Appendices
ROELLECOURT	4.4.17		Major Stevenson reported sick. Capt. Yates, AVC received instructions from him to carry on during temporary absence, received wire from DHQ that 37th MVS should move to DUISANS	
"	5.4.17		DHQ moved to AGNES. Weather most favourable, no mishaps reported.	
AGNEZ	6.4.17		Went over to HARDAREQ and interviewed Major Pallin ADVS 15 Division re proposed advanced mobile section. Fragment of shell struck office door opposite my office. Signed correspondence & returns etc. The wet	
	7.4.17		Signed weather conditions much improved. Met ADVS 15 Division and selected suitable place for advanced MVS. Also asked Q office for approval.	
"	8.4.17		Wrote to ADVS. Signed correspondence, nothing of importance to record.	
"	9.4.17		MAJOR J. R. STEEVENSON AVC returned from 12 Stationary Hospital & resumed duties of ADVS	JS
"	10.4.17		Visited MVS at DUISANS. Advanced collecting post established on Race Course. W of ARRAS.	JS
"	11.4.17		Visited Transport of Infty Bdes at BLANGY. E of ARRAS	JS
"	12.4.17		To MVS. Office routine	JS
"	13.4.17		Usual Routine.	JS

A5834 Wt. W4973/M687 750,000 8/16 D. D. & L. Ltd. Forms/C.2118/13

Instructions regarding War Diaries and Intelligence Summaries are contained in F. S. Regs., Part II. and the Staff Manual respectively. Title pages will be prepared in manuscript.

WAR DIARY
or
INTELLIGENCE SUMMARY.
(Erase heading not required.)

Army Form C. 2118.

Place	Date	Hour	Summary of Events and Information	Remarks and references to Appendices
LIGNEREUIL	14.4.17		March from AGNEZ-LES-DUISANS to LIGNEREUIL. M.V.S. also at latter place. Notified D.D.V.S. 3rd Army to that effect.	[initials]
"	15.4.17		Inspected transport animals of 112th Infty Bde & 112th M.G. Coy. Also No 4 Coy 37th Div. Train	[initials]
"	16.4.17		Inspected transport animals of 63rd Infty Bde & 63rd M.G. Coy & No 2 Coy 37th Div. Train.	[initials]
"	17.4.17		Inspected 2.3 & 4 Coys 37th Div. Train with O.C. To M.V.S.	[initials]
"	18.4.17		Inspected animals of 4th Middlesex Regt & 8th Lincoln Regt. Received a wire to be prepared to move to-morrow	[initials]
"	19.4.17		To M.V.S. Usual Routine	
"	20.4.17		Received to go move on 21st inst.	
"	21.4.17		Marched to ETRUN near ARRAS. 28 M.V.S. at ETRUN. Took over from 4th DIVISION force stables	[initials]

A5834 Wt. W4973/M687 750,000 8/16 D. D. & L. Ltd. Forms/C.2118/13

Army Form C. 2118.

Instructions regarding War Diaries and Intelligence Summaries are contained in F. S. Regs., Part II, and the Staff Manual respectively. Title pages will be prepared in manuscript.

WAR DIARY
or
INTELLIGENCE SUMMARY.

(Erase heading not required.)

ASSISTANT DIRECTOR OF VETERINARY SERVICES — DIVISION. No. 1?? Date 15/?

Place	Date	Hour	Summary of Events and Information	Remarks and references to Appendices
ETRUN	22.4.17		Inspected Infty Bde Transport at ST. NICHOLAS. Placed an advanced collecting post near them. 28 M.V.S took over 1 N.C.O + 10 men to act as conducting parties from the 4th Division M.V.S.	J.S.
"	23.4.17		To M.V.S + usual routine	
"	24.4.17		To visit Infty Transport at ST NICHOLAS + to see change of G.S.O.2. To M.V.S.	J.S.
"	25.4.17		Received orders for Rear D.H.Q to proceed to ARRAS on 26/4/17	J.
ARRAS	26.4.17		Moved to ARRAS with Rear echelon D.H.Q. Office situated in RUE des AUGUSTINES. Informed DDVS 3rd Army & V o/c units.	J.S.
			Sergt Warburton A.V.C. joined from A/123/RFA Short term to 28 M.V.S to be dispatched to his unit on 27.4.17. 28 M.V.S to remain at ETRUN for the present.	J.S.

A5834 Wt. W4973/M687 750,000 8/16 D. D. & L. Ltd. Forms/C.2118/13

Instructions regarding War Diaries and Intelligence Summaries are contained in F. S. Regs., Part II. and the Staff Manual respectively. Title pages will be prepared in manuscript.

WAR DIARY
or
INTELLIGENCE SUMMARY.
(Erase heading not required.)

Army Form C. 2118.

Place	Date	Hour	Summary of Events and Information	Remarks and references to Appendices
ARRAS	27.4.17		Visited Transport of Infty Bdes, & saw wounded animals. Also advanced collecting post.	J.
"	28.4.17		To M.V.S at ETRUN & to advanced collecting post. Despatched weekly states.	J.
"	29.4.17		To Infty Transport & advanced collect: post. Saw O.C M.V.S & Capt HUSTON A.V.C. Received orders to move with D.H.Q to LIGNEREUIL on 30th inst. Issued orders to 28 M.V.S to move as soon as the sick animals have been evacuated.	J.
LIGNEREUIL	30.4.17		Marched fm ARRAS to LIGNEREUIL. 28th M.V.S left behind at ETRUN with orders to rejoin the division on 1.5.17 after evacuating sick animals at AGNEZ	J.

J. Hennessy Major
ADVS
34 Division

A5834 Wt. W4973/M687 750,000 8/16 D. D. & L. Ltd. Forms/C.2118/13

Instructions regarding War Diaries and Intelligence Summaries are contained in F. S. Regs., Part II. and the Staff Manual respectively. Title pages will be prepared in manuscript.

WAR DIARY
or
INTELLIGENCE SUMMARY.
(Erase heading not required.)

A.D.V.S.
37th Divn

Vol 22

Army Form C. 2118.

Place	Date	Hour	Summary of Events and Information	Remarks and references to Appendices
LIGNEREUIL	1.5.17		Visited 63rd Bde H.Q. & transport of 4th Middlesex. & 63rd M.G. Coy & 152 Coy R.E. 28 M.V.S. marched from ETRUN to LIGNEREUIL	
"	2.5.17		Visited 153rd Coy R.E. 6th Bedfords & B Echelon D.A.C	J.C.
"	3.5.17		Visited 154 Coy R.E. & 10th R.F. Usual routine	J.C.
"	4.5.17		Visited 9th North Staffords (Pioneers) & 112 M.G. Coy & 11th Warwicks.	
"	5.5.17		Accompanied G.C. Divl Train to inspect 48, 49th & 50th Field ambulances. Horses & Mules looking fit & well.	J
"	6.5.17		To M.V.S. Prepared fresh ~~statement of~~ weekly state for D.D.V.S. 3rd Army including all attached units in one state.	J.C.
"	7.5.17		Accompanied Divisional Commander to inspect the R.A. 37th Divn at present attached 21st Division. Found horses etc in fairly satisfactory condition but 364 animals under strength.	

A5834 Wt. W4973/M687 750,000 8/16 D. D. & L. Ltd. Forms/C.2118/13

Army Form C. 2118.

Instructions regarding War Diaries and Intelligence Summaries are contained in F. S. Regs., Part II. and the Staff Manual respectively. Title pages will be prepared in manuscript.

WAR DIARY
or
INTELLIGENCE SUMMARY.
(Erase heading not required.)

Place	Date	Hour	Summary of Events and Information	Remarks and references to Appendices
LIGNEREUIL	8.5.17		Accompanied O.C. 37th Div. Train & inspect Transport of 111 M.G. Coy & 13th Rifle Bde. Shoeing of former requires a lot more attention	[illegible]
"	9.5.17		Judged at Divisional Transport Competition	[illegible]
"	10.5.17		Accompanied O.C. 37th Div. Train & inspect transport of 63rd Infy Bde. Shoeing unsatisfactory in 10 York & Lancs & 63rd M.G. Coy especially so in latter.	[illegible]
"	11.5.17		Accompanied O.C. 37 Train & inspect 112th Infy Bde & 112 M.G. Coy. Prepared weekly states	[illegible]
"	12.5.17		Dispatched weekly states. Inspected B. Echelon 37 D.A.C.	[illegible]
"	13.5.17		[illegible] Dog Show.	[illegible]
"	14.5.17		Went to Abbeville & saw the 22 & 5 Vety Hospitals. Called on D.V.S.	[illegible]

A5834 Wt. W4973/M687 750,000 8/16 D. D. & L. Ltd. Forms/C.2118/13

Instructions regarding War Diaries and Intelligence Summaries are contained in F. S. Regs., Part II. and the Staff Manual respectively. Title pages will be prepared in manuscript.

WAR DIARY
or
INTELLIGENCE SUMMARY.
(Erase heading not required.)

Army Form C. 2118.

Place	Date	Hour	Summary of Events and Information	Remarks and references to Appendices
LIGNEREUIL	15.5.17		To M.V.S & usual routine.	[illegible]
"	16.5.17		Inspected animals of 49th Field Ambulance & 153 Coy R E & visited 15th Div: H.Q at LE CAUROY to arrange with A.D.V.S re handing over a few animals from 28 M.V.S to 24th M.V.S in the event of the Division moving in a few days.	[illegible]
			Afterwards attended at a demonstration by Div: Gas Officer on the fitting of gas respirators on horses at 28 M.V.S All V.O's & Sergts A.V.C attended & Transport Officers & N.C.O's of units of the division	[illegible]
"	17.5.17		To M.V.S Usual routine	[illegible]
"	18.5.17		Saw Divisional Supply Transport on the March. Orders to proceed to WARLUS on 19th inst. Issued orders to 28 M.V.S to move to Warlus on 19th inst.	[illegible]
WARLUS.	19.5.17		Moved with D.H.Q to WARLUS. Also 28 M.V.S. Notified ~~A.D.V~~ D.D.V.S Third Army of move	[illegible]
"	20.5.17		Usual routine.	

A5834 Wt. W4973/M687 750,000 8/16 D. D. & L. Ltd. Forms/C.2118/13

Instructions regarding War Diaries and Intelligence Summaries are contained in F. S. Regs., Part II. and the Staff Manual respectively. Title pages will be prepared in manuscript.

WAR DIARY
or
INTELLIGENCE SUMMARY.
(Erase heading not required.)

Army Form C. 2118.

Place	Date	Hour	Summary of Events and Information	Remarks and references to Appendices
WARLUS ARRAS	21.5.17.		Moved to ARRAS. 28 M.V.S located at FAUBOURG D'AMIENS on west side of ARRAS. Took over vety administration of 3rd Field Survey Coy RE 133 A.T. Coy R.E. 232 Army Field Artillery + 15th Div: Artillery from ADVS 56th Division	
ARRAS	22.5.17		To M.V.S + usual routine.	
"	23.5.17		Visited 63rd Infty Bde Transport + No 2 Coy 39 Train. To M.V.S	
"	24.5.17		To M.V.S. 19 cases of severe sarcoptic Mange admitted to M.V.S from 14 Heavy Battery + 35 Heavy Battery. Reported same to D.D.V.S. 3 Army	
"	25.5.17		Conference of V.Os. Preparing weekly states. 10 mules + 3 Riders killed + 8 mules wounded by shell in 153 FIELD Coy R.E. ARRAS shelled by a H.V. Gun. Shells also fell near M.V.S	
"	26.5.17		Despatched weekly states. Applied to D.D.V.S 3rd Army for assistance to the M.V.S i.e. a conducting party to be attached.	
"	27.5.17		Usual routine	
"	28.5.17		Visited Infty transport + M.V.S.	
"	29.5.17		Visited 12th D.A.C	
"	30.5.17 / 31.5.17		Usual routine. Received orders to move on 2.6.17 to LIGNEREUIL.	

[illegible] Major
ADVS 37 Division

Vol 23

SECRET

War Diary

A.D.V.S.

3rd Division

JUNE 1917

Instructions regarding War Diaries and Intelligence Summaries are contained in F. S. Regs., Part II. and the Staff Manual respectively. Title pages will be prepared in manuscript.

WAR DIARY
or
INTELLIGENCE SUMMARY.
(Erase heading not required.)

Army Form C. 2118.

Place	Date	Hour	Summary of Events and Information	Remarks and references to Appendices
ARRAS	1.6.17		Conference of V.O's Preparing weekly state. D.D.V.S. 3rd called & afternoons inspected 20 M.V.S.	[initials]
LIGNEREUIL	2.6.17		Marched to LIGNEREUIL. 20 M.V.S. to same place	[initials]
"	3.6.17		Attended conference of A.D's V.S. at office of D.D.V.S. 3rd Army	[initials]
"	4.6.17		Inspected Infty Transport & Usual routine	
"	5.6.17		To B. Echelon D.A.C. Reported to D.D.V.S. 3rd Army on mules there & was of opinion that an intermediate size is required between Nos 15 & 16 sizes.	[initials]
"	6.6.17		To BOMY & selected site for M.V.S at LUGY about 16 miles S.W. of St. Omer.	[initials]
"	7.6.17		M.V.S moved to VALHOUN en route to LUGY.	[initials]
BOMY	8.6.17		Arrived at BOMY with D.H.Q.	[initials]
"	9.6.17		Usual routine. Saw V.O's & despatched weekly state to D.D.V.S. First Army. D.D.V.S. First Army & D.D.R. called at office.	[initials]

Instructions regarding War Diaries and Intelligence Summaries are contained in F. S. Regs., Part II. and the Staff Manual respectively. Title pages will be prepared in manuscript.

WAR DIARY
or
INTELLIGENCE SUMMARY.
(*Erase heading not required.*)

Army Form C. 2118.

Place	Date	Hour	Summary of Events and Information	Remarks and references to Appendices
BOMY.	10.6.17		Visited 63rd Infty Bde at FRUGES	[initials]
"	11.6.17		Usual routine	
"	12.6.17 to 16.6.17		Usual routine Despatched weekly states to D.D.V.S First Army on 16.6.17	[initials]
"	18.6.17 to 19.6.17		Took over duties of A.D.V.S (Capt Huston) Major Stevenson being on leave	[initials]
"	20.6.17 to 22.6.17		Usual duties signed reports.	[initials]
"	23.6.17		Moved with my own unit and handed over duties of ADVS to Captain Yates as the Division was on the move.	[initials]
STEENBEQUE	24.6.17		Moved with H.Q. to this place yesterday (Capt Yates) took over duties of ADVS from Capt Huston, weather fine for move	[initials]
LOCRE	25.6.17		H.Q. MVS + Signals arrived at this place yesterday long march all animals seemed to have done well	[initials]
"	26.6.17 to 29.6.17		Visited various units + attended animals attached to H.Q. Signed returns to DDVS. Visited Corps D.I.P. also Corps Veterinary Depot. Usual duties	[initials]
DRANOUTRE	30.6.17		D.H.Q moved to DRANOUTRE. Major J. R. Stevenson ADVS rejoined Division from 10 days leave of absence to England. 36th Div. Arty attached to Division.	[initials]

A5834 Wt. W4973/ 750,000 8/16 D. D. & L. Ltd. Forms/C.2118/13.

Vol 24

War Diary

D.A.D.V.S. 37th Divn

July 1917

Instructions regarding War Diaries and Intelligence Summaries are contained in F. S. Regs., Part II. and the Staff Manual respectively. Title pages will be prepared in manuscript.

WAR DIARY
or
INTELLIGENCE SUMMARY.
(Erase heading not required.)

D.A.D.V.S., 37TH DIVISION.
No.........
Date.........

Army Form C. 2118.

Place	Date	Hour	Summary of Events and Information	Remarks and references to Appendices
DRANOUTRE	1.7.17		To M.V.S. & to see ADVS IX Corps. MVS at LOCRE	[illegible]
	2.7.17		Went to IX Corps Dip at St: JANS CAPPEL & saw B & D 153 RFA, 36 DIV: ARTY horses being put through. Visited IX Corps MVS at HAEGEDORNE. 1 Sergt: & 3 MEN of 37. M.V.S. attached to IX Corps M.V.S.	[illegible]
	3.7.17		Accompanied Divisional Commander to inspect transport of 111 Infty Bde. Usual routine	[illegible]
	4.7.17		Usual routine.	
	5.7.17			
	6.7.17		Preparing weekly states & usual routine	[illegible]
	7.7.17		Took weekly states to ADVS IX Corps. Usual routine	[illegible]
	8.7.17		Routine	
	9.7.17		ADVS IX Corps visited transport lines of infty units — the Division & Field Ambulances	[illegible]
	10.7.17		37: Div Arty rejoined division after being absent since March 1917. Horses of same in very fair condition	[illegible]

A5834 Wt. W4973/ 750,000 8/16 D. D. & L. Ltd. Forms/C.2118/13.

Instructions regarding War Diaries and Intelligence Summaries are contained in F. S. Regs., Part II. and the Staff Manual respectively. Title pages will be prepared in manuscript.

WAR DIARY
or
INTELLIGENCE SUMMARY.
(Erase heading not required.)

D.A.D.V.S.,
37TH DIVISION.
No.............
Date...........

Army Form C. 2118.

Place	Date	Hour	Summary of Events and Information	Remarks and references to Appendices
DRANOUTRE	11.7.17		Visited waggon lines of R.A units + usual routine. Capt. H. Jewell AVC ordered to report to No 23 Vety Hospital at ST. OMER on reduction of establishment of V.O's of a division.	J.S.
"	12.7.17		Visited waggon lines of 124/Bde R.F.A with Capt. Spurr AVC	J.S.
"	13.7.17		Capt. H. Jewell AVC left for No 23 Vety Hospital. Reported his departure to A.D.V.S. IX Corps + to 37th DIV Q. Prepared weekly states. Conference of V.O's in the evening. Capt. R.S.L. Beaumont AVC left on 10 days leave to England. Reported his departure to ADVS IX Corps.	J.S.
"	14.7.17		Usual routine. Conference of DADsVS at office of ADVS IX Corps at 3.0 p.m.	J.S.
"	15.7.17		Usual routine	J.S.
"	16.7.17		do do	J.S.
"	17.7.17		ADVS IX Corps inspected horses of 37th DIV ARTY.	
"	18.7.17		No 1 + 2 Sec: DAC + C + D/123 + B/124 horses sent their horses through the IX Corps Horse Dip at ST JANS CAPELLE	J.S.

A5834 Wt. W4973/M... 750,000 8/16 D. D. & L. Ltd. Forms/C.2118/13.

Instructions regarding War Diaries and Intelligence Summaries are contained in F. S. Regs., Part II. and the Staff Manual respectively. Title pages will be prepared in manuscript.

WAR DIARY
or
INTELLIGENCE SUMMARY.
(Erase heading not required.)

D.A.D.V.S.,
37TH DIVISION.
No.............
Date...........

Army Form C. 2118.

Place	Date	Hour	Summary of Events and Information	Remarks and references to Appendices
DRANOUTRE	19.7.17.		Conference of V.O's. Usual Routine	[illegible]
"	20.7.17		Prepared & despatched weekly states.	[illegible]
"	21.7.17		Attended at office of ADVS IX Corps. Usual routine	[illegible]
"			Accompanied Divisional Commander to inspect waggon lines of A/124 & B/124 R.F.A	
"	22.7.17 } 26.7.17 }		Usual routine. Passed Horses of No 1, 2 & 3 Sect. DAC & C/124 & B/124 through IX Corps Horse clip.	[illegible]
"	27.7.17		Prepared & despatched weekly states	[illegible]
"	28.7.17		Attended at office of ADVS IX Corps.	
"	29.7.17		Usual routine	[illegible]
"	31.7.17			

[illegible signature]
Major. AVC
DADVS 37 DIV.

A5834 Wt. W4973/[illegible] 750,000 8/16 D. D. & L. Ltd. Forms/C.2118/13.

Vol 25

War Diary

D.A.D.V.S.

57th Div

Aug 1917.

Instructions regarding War Diaries and Intelligence Summaries are contained in F. S. Regs., Part II. and the Staff Manual respectively. Title pages will be prepared in manuscript.

WAR DIARY
or
INTELLIGENCE SUMMARY.
(Erase heading not required.)

Army Form C. 2118.

Place	Date	Hour	Summary of Events and Information	Remarks and references to Appendices
DRANOUTRE	1.8.17		Usual routine	[illegible]
	2.8.17		Conference of V.Os of DIVISION.	[illegible]
	3.8.17		Prepared & despatched weekly states.	[illegible]
	4.8.17		Attended conference at office of ADVS IX Corps. Usual routine	[illegible]
	5.8.17 to 7.8.17		Usual routine	[illegible]
SCHERPENBURG	8.8.17		DHQ moved to Scherpenburg via: LOCRE 28 M.V.S. to LOCRE. Handed over attached units to DADVS 4th Australian Division. Took over same attached units from 19th DIVISION.	[illegible]
"	9.8.17		Usual routine.	
"	10.8.17 to 17.8.17		Usual routine. Accompanied on these days the IX Corps Horse Advisor & Div: Horse Advisor to select Brood Mares, the same to be branded on the near cheek & sent to England after the war.	[illegible]
"	18.8.17 to 24.8.17		Usual routine. On 24th prepared & despatched weekly states to ADVS IX Corps	[illegible]
"	25.8.17		Attended conference of DADVS at office of IX Corps ADVS	
"	26.8.17 to 27.8.17		Usual routine	[illegible]

A5834 Wt. W4973/M687 750,000 8/16 D. D. & L. Ltd. Forms/C.2118/13.

Instructions regarding War Diaries and Intelligence Summaries are contained in F. S. Regs., Part II. and the Staff Manual respectively. Title pages will be prepared in manuscript.

WAR DIARY

or

INTELLIGENCE SUMMARY.

(Erase heading not required.)

Army Form C. 2118.

Place	Date	Hour	Summary of Events and Information	Remarks and references to Appendices
SCHERPENBERG	28.8.17		Accompanied Divisional Commander to inspect 2.3 & 4 Coys 37th Div: Train & afterwards to AA & QMG 37 DIV: to inspect Transport of 111th Infantry Bde	
"	29.8.17		Accompanied ADVS IX Corps & Corps Horse Examiner to inspect animals of C/123/Bde R.F.A	
"	30.8.17		Conference of V.O's.	
"	31.8.17		Despatched weekly states etc to ADVS IX Corps.	

[illegible signature]
Major
D.A.D.V.S
37TH DIVISION

A5834 Wt. W4973/M687 750,000 8/16 D. D. & L. Ltd. Forms/C.2118/13.

War Diary

D.A.D.V.S. 37th Divn

Sept 1917

Vol 26

17

Instructions regarding War Diaries and Intelligence Summaries are contained in F. S. Regs., Part II. and the Staff Manual respectively. Title pages will be prepared in manuscript.

WAR DIARY
or
INTELLIGENCE SUMMARY.
(*Erase heading not required.*)

Army Form C. 2118.

Place	Date	Hour	Summary of Events and Information	Remarks and references to Appendices
SCHERPENBERG	1.9.17		Conference of DADsVS at office of ADVS. IX Corps.	JS
"	2.9.17 to 6.9.17		Usual routine. ADVS IX Corps inspected horses of C/124/RFA. C/123/RFA & D/123/RFA	
"	7-9-17		Conference at my office of V.O's of the division. Usual routine. Despatched weekly states to ADVS IX Corps	JS
"	8.9.17		Conference of DADsVS at office of ADVS IX Corps.	JS
"	9-9-17		Ordered 28 M.VS to move to ST JANS CAPPEL on afternoon of 10th & to take over there from 31st MVS 19 Division who are relieving 28 M.VS at LOCRE.	JS
"	10.9.17 to 11.9.17		Usual routine	JS
ST JANS CAPPEL	12.9.17		DHQ moved to ST. JANS CAPPEL	JS

A5834 Wt. W4973/M687 750,000 8/16 D. D. & L. Ltd. Forms/C.2118/13.

Instructions regarding War Diaries and Intelligence Summaries are contained in F. S. Regs., Part II. and the Staff Manual respectively. Title pages will be prepared in manuscript.

WAR DIARY
or
INTELLIGENCE SUMMARY.
(Erase heading not required.)

Army Form C. 2118.

Place	Date	Hour	Summary of Events and Information	Remarks and references to Appendices
ST. JANS CAPPEL	13.9.17		Conference of V.Os of Division. 49th Div: Arty & 4th Div: Arty attached for administration	J.S.
"	14.9.17		Usual routine	J.S.
"	15.9.17		Conference of A.D.V.S of Divisions at office of A.D.V.S IX Corps	J.S.
"	16.9.17		Accompanied G.O.C 37th Div to inspect 152, 153 & 154 Field Coys R.E.	J.S.
"	17.9.17 – 19.9.17		Usual routine.	J.S.
"	20.9.17		Conference of V.Os & preparing weekly states	J.S.
"	21.9.17		Usual routine	
"	22.9.17		Attended conference at office of A.D.V.S IX Corps.	J.S.
"	23 & 24.9.17		Usual routine	J.S.
	25.9.17		Divisional Horse Show.	J.S.

A5834 Wt. W4973/M687 750,000 8/16 D. D. & L. Ltd. Forms/C.2118/13.

Army Form C. 2118.

WAR DIARY
or
INTELLIGENCE SUMMARY.
(Erase heading not required.)

Instructions regarding War Diaries and Intelligence Summaries are contained in F. S. Regs., Part II. and the Staff Manual respectively. Title pages will be prepared in manuscript.

Place	Date	Hour	Summary of Events and Information	Remarks and references to Appendices
ST JANS CAPPEL	26-27/9/17		Usual routine.	[illegible]
"	28.9.17		DHQ moved to ZEVECOTEN nr RENINGHELST	
ZEVECOTEN	29.9.17		25 MVS moved from ST JANS CAPPEL to LA CLYTTE & relieved MVS of 39th Division. Visited ADVS IX Corps.	[illegible]
"	30.9.17		Usual routine	[illegible]

[signature] Major
DADVS 34 DIV.

A5834 Wt. W4973/M687 750,000 8/16 D. D. & L. Ltd. Forms/C.2118/13.

Vol 27

War Diary

D.A.D.V.S. 37th Division

Oct 1917.

Army Form C. 2118.

Instructions regarding War Diaries and Intelligence Summaries are contained in F. S. Regs., Part II. and the Staff Manual respectively. Title pages will be prepared in manuscript.

WAR DIARY
or
INTELLIGENCE SUMMARY.

(Erase heading not required.)

Place	Date	Hour	Summary of Events and Information	Remarks and references to Appendices
DE ZON CAMP	1.10.17		Moved with DHQ to DE ZON Camp near LA CLYTTE	[illegible]
"	2.10.17 to 5.10.17		Usual routine	[illegible]
"	6.10.17		Attended conference at ADVS Office IX Corps. Took weekly states	[illegible]
"	7.10.17 to 12.10.17		30 animals died from shell wounds during the week, many wounded. Cases mostly all occurred in pack animals taking up rations at night. On 12.10.17 attended conference with DDVS 2nd Army. Saw model clipping establishment at WESTOUTRE but power machinery was not ready for a demonstration.	[illegible]
	13.10.17		Attended at offices of ADVS IX Corps with weekly states.	
	14.10.17		Usual routine. Granted leave to England from 16.10.17 to 26.10.17. CAPT. J H YATES (O.C. 20 M.V.S.) to perform my duties during my absence. Notified ADVS IX Corps to that effect.	[illegible]

A5834 Wt. W4973/M687 750,000 8/16 D. D. & L. Ltd. Forms/C.2118/13.

Instructions regarding War Diaries and Intelligence Summaries are contained in F. S. Regs., Par. II, and the Staff Manual respectively. Title pages will be prepared in manuscript.

WAR DIARY
or
INTELLIGENCE SUMMARY.
(Erase heading not required.)

Army Form C. 2118.

Place	Date	Hour	Summary of Events and Information	Remarks and references to Appendices
16-10-17	DE ZON.		~~[illegible]~~ HQ moved to St JAN CAPEL. this morning. Major Stevenson went on leave. took over duties of DADVS	[illegible]
17-10-17 to 20-10-17	St JAN CAPEL.	"	Nothing unusual occured. signed returns and visited HQ stables & usual routine work. Called to see ADVS Corps & accompanied him to LOCRE to inspect clipping shed	[illegible]
21 10 17 to 26. 10.17	"	"	Saw DAQMS re clipping shed also Engineers. also Consulted with A.D.V.S Corps re same. Made start on 24th clipping stopped by order of A/Divisional General restarted on 26. Signed returns 28th MVS moved to ~~[illegible]~~ SCHAEXKEN. Weather very wet	[illegible]
27-10-17	"		Major J. R. Stevenson returned from leave to England & resumed duties of DADVS from Capt. J. H. Yates	[illegible]
28-10-17 to 31-10-17	"		Usual routine.	[illegible]

A6945 Wt. W11422/M1160 350,000 12/16 D. D. & L. Forms/C./2118/14.

19

Instructions regarding War Diaries and Intelligence Summaries are contained in F. S. Regs., Part II, and the Staff Manual respectively. Title pages will be prepared in manuscript.

WAR DIARY
or
INTELLIGENCE SUMMARY.
(Erase heading not required.)

D.A.D.V.S
37TH DIVISION

Army Form C. 2118.

Vol 28

Place	Date	Hour	Summary of Events and Information	Remarks and references to Appendices
ST JANS CAPPEL	1.11.17 to 9.11.17		Usual routine	[illegible]
SCHERPENBERG	10.11.17		D.H.Q. moved to SCHERPENBERG & took over from 19th DIVISION	
"	11.11.17 to 30.11.17		Usual routine. Commenced clipping of horses of Division on 30.11.17. Only mules remain to be done. Divisional clipping Establishment works well & is clipping is quicker & more satisfactory than when done by units. Received instructions to evacuate all severe cases of Ophthalmia to Base, & treat slight cases in M.V.S by injecting 1 C.C. of Lugol's solution into ~~[illegible]~~ sub-orbital fat every 10th day.	

[illegible signature]
Brig.

D.A.D.V.S
37TH DIVISION

A5834 Wt. W4973/M687 750,000 8/16 D. D. & L. Ltd. Forms/C.2118/13.

Instructions regarding War Diaries and Intelligence Summaries are contained in F. S. Regs., Part II. and the Staff Manual respectively. Title pages will be prepared in manuscript.

WAR DIARY
or
~~INTELLIGENCE SUMMARY.~~
(Erase heading not required.)

Army Form C. 2118.

D.A D.V.S
37TH DIVISION

Vol 29

Place	Date	Hour	Summary of Events and Information	Remarks and references to Appendices
SCHERPENBERG				
	1.12.17		Attended Conference at ADVS. office IX Corps	
	2.12.17 to 6.12.17		Took over duties of ADVS IX Corps during his absence on leave.	
	6.12.17		Capt. W. HUSTON. A.V.C. was accidentally killed by a motor lorry on the LOCRE KEMMEL road.	
	7.12.17		Office routine.	
	8.12.17		Attended Conference at ADVS office IX Corps.	
	9.12.17 to 10.12.17		Usual routine. 10.12.17. Inspected animals evacuated today by road.	
	11.12.17		Sealed and despatched Kit and Effects of Capt. W. HUSTON. A.V.C. to D.A.G. G.H.Q. 3rd Echelon (Canadian Section Effects Branch)	
	12.12.17 to 14.12.17		Inspected animals of 123 and 124 Bdes R.F.A., and arranged for the dipping of 50 animals during the coming week. 13.12.17. Clipping Depot at KRABBENHOF FARM closed for the season. Total number clipped at this establishment 1607 Horses. 708 Mules.	
	14.12.17		28th M.V.S. moved from LA CLYTTE to KRABBENHOF FARM, near LOCRE.	
	15.12.17		Attended Conference at ADVS. office IX Corps. Took weekly States.	
	16.12.17 to 18.12.17		Usual routine. 16.12.17 Lieut. J. CRAIG. A.V.C. joined 37th DIVN from No 2. Veterinary Hospital HAVRE.	

D. D. & L., London, E.C.
(A8004) Wt. W1771/M2031 750,000 5/17 Sch. 52 Forms/C2118/14

Instructions regarding War Diaries and Intelligence Summaries are contained in F. S. Regs., Part II. and the Staff Manual respectively. Title pages will be prepared in manuscript.

WAR DIARY
or
~~INTELLIGENCE SUMMARY.~~
(Erase heading not required.)

Army Form C. 2118.

D.A D.V.S
37TH DIVISION

Place	Date	Hour	Summary of Events and Information	Remarks and references to Appendices
SCHERPENBERG	19.12.17		Inspected animals at 28th MVS for evacuation today from OUDERDOM Railhead	
	20.12.17 to 22.12.17		Usual routine 22.12.17 Attended Conference at A.D.V.S. office IX Corps. Received D.V.S. instructions. No 12/3792/17 dated 19.12.17 requesting a seperation in all Returns for horses, from those for mules.	
	23.12.17		10 Men of the 28th M.V.S. (class A) were sent to BASE for transfer. These men were replaced by 10 others on the 21/12/17 from No 2 Veterinary Hospital HAVRE.	
	24.12.17		Inspected animals for evacuation today via OUDERDOM Railhead. Also those of No 2 Section DAC, 123 and 124 Bdes R.F.A.	
	25.12.17 to 27.12.17		Usual routine. 28.12.17 Inspected animals for evacuation today via OUDERDOM Railhead of 123 Bde and 247 M. G. Co.	
	29.12.17		19th Divn Artillery moved out of IX Corps area Inspected animals of 37th Divl Train (4 Coys)	
	30.12.17		D.D.V.S. 2nd Army visited 28th M.V.S.	
	31.12.17		Office routine	

J Stevens [?] Major

D.A.D.V.S
37TH DIVISION

(A8004) D. D. & L., London, E.C. Wt. W1771/M2731 750,000 5/17 Sch. 52 Forms/C2118/14

DDVS 37th Divn

WAR DIARY
or
INTELLIGENCE SUMMARY.
(Erase heading not required.)

Army Form C. 2118.

Instructions regarding War Diaries and Intelligence Summaries are contained in F. S. Regs., Part II. and the Staff Manual respectively. Title pages will be prepared in manuscript.

Vol 30

Place	Date	Hour	Summary of Events and Information	Remarks and references to Appendices
SCHERPENBERG				
	1/1/18 to 3/1/18		Usual Routine	
	4/1/18		Attended conference at ADVS office IX Corps. Took weekly Returns	
	5/1/18		DDR Fourth Army cast 16 animals of 37th Divl Units	
	6/1/18		Inspected animals of 37th Divl Train	
	7/1/18 to 10/1/18		Usual Routine	
	11/1/18		Forwarded Weekly Returns to IX Corps. 28 MVS moved by road to RACQUINGHEM.	
	12/1/18		D.H.Q. moved to Rest Area, BLARINGHEM. No SE6600 P/A/Sgt HAYES D/123 Bde evacuated sick	
BLARINGHEM	13/1/18		Animals cast by DDR Fourth Army were evacuated	
	14/1/18		Inspected animals of D.H.Q.	
	13/1/18		Capt. J H YATES returned from Leave	
	15/1/18 to 17/1/18		Usual Routine	
	18/1/18		Forwarded weekly Returns to ADVS IX Corps.	
	19/1/18 to 22/1/18		Usual Routine.	

D. D. & L., London, E.C.
(A8004) Wt. W1771/M2 31 750,000 5/17 Sch. 32 Forms/C2118/14

Army Form C. 2118.

WAR DIARY
or
INTELLIGENCE SUMMARY.
(Erase heading not required.)

Instructions regarding War Diaries and Intelligence Summaries are contained in F. S. Regs., Part II. and the Staff Manual respectively. Title pages will be prepared in manuscript.

Place	Date	Hour	Summary of Events and Information	Remarks and references to Appendices
BLARINGHEM	23/1/17.		Major Stevenson proceeded on 14 days leave. assumed duties of DADVS inspected horses prior to evacuation to Base.	[illegible]
	24/1/18		Visited offices and inspected animals of DHQ	[illegible]
	25/1/18		Office routine. G.O.C reported Farrier Sergeant of 152 R.E. also inspected that unit	[illegible]
	26/1/18 to 28/1/18		Usual routine duties saw AAQMG re distribution of exchange of horses of units being detached from division also saw O.C 37 Train re, same	[illegible]
	29/1/18		Office routine. Visited HQ animals A.P.M. horse bad with an acute attack of Colic	[illegible]
	30/1/18		Inspected animals prior to evacuation to base usual office routine	[illegible]
	31/1/18		Visited H.Q animals A.P.M. horse had a return of his attacks & eventually died from displacement of bowels.	

Snottyfale Cupl AVC [illegible]
A/DADVS 37th Divn

D. D. & L., London, E.C.
(A8004) Wt. W1771/M2 31 750,000 5/17 Sch. 52 Forms/C2118/14

16

Instructions regarding War Diaries and Intelligence Summaries are contained in F. S. Regs., Part II. and the Staff Manual respectively. Title pages will be prepared in manuscript.

WAR DIARY
or
INTELLIGENCE SUMMARY.

(Erase heading not required.)

D.A.D.V.S
87TH DIVISION

Army Form C. 2118.

Vol 31

Place	Date	Hour	Summary of Events and Information	Remarks and references to Appendices
BLARINGHEM.	1-2-18		Office routine returns completed and despatched to A.D.V.S IX corps.	
"	2-2-18.		Inspected D.H.Q animals Signal Co.	
"	3-2-18 to 5-2-18		Called at DADVS office daily signed correspondence & the inspected [illegible] animals for evacuation. Weather conditions mild and fine	
"	6.2.18		Major J R Stevenson returned from leave to England & resumed duties of DADVS.	
"	7.2.18. to 15.2.18		Usual routine	
	16.2.18		28 M.V.S marched to STRAZEELE & thence on 17th to WESTOUTRE & took over standing vacated by 20th DIV: M.V.S.	
	17.2.18		D.H.Q moved to WESTOUTRE. Informed ADVS XXII Corps of location of my office & took over veterinary administration of various units handed over to me by DADVS 20th DIV.	

D. D. & L., London, E.C. (A8004) Wt. W1771/M2 31 750,000 5/17 Sch. 52 Forms/C2118/14

Instructions regarding War Diaries and Intelligence Summaries are contained in F. S. Regs., Part II. and the Staff Manual respectively. Title pages will be prepared in manuscript.

WAR DIARY
or
INTELLIGENCE SUMMARY.

(Erase heading not required.)

D.A.D.V.S
37TH DIVISION

Army Form C. 2118.

Place	Date	Hour	Summary of Events and Information	Remarks and references to Appendices
WESTOUTRE	18	2 18	Inspected DIV Arty. animals & usual routine	EP
	19	2 18	Usual routine	
	to 24	2 18		
ANZAC CAMP	25	2 18	DHQ moved to ANZAC CAMP between DICKEBUSCH & YPRES.	21
	26	2 18	Usual routine. Very few sick animals & no disease of importance except about 12 cases of Ophthalmia in the division	
	27	2/18	} Usual routine	
	28	2/18		

J Stevens
Major

D.A.D.V.S
37TH DIVISION

(A8004) D. D. & L., London, E.C. Wt. W1771/M2031 750,000 5/17 Sch. 52 Forms/C2118/14

16

Army Form C. 2118.

WAR DIARY
or
INTELLIGENCE SUMMARY.
(Erase heading not required.)

Instructions regarding War Diaries and Intelligence Summaries are contained in F. S. Regs., Part II. and the Staff Manual respectively. Title pages will be prepared in manuscript.

D.A.D.V.S
37TH DIVISION

Vol 32

Place	Date	Hour	Summary of Events and Information	Remarks and references to Appendices
ANZAC CAMP between Dickebusch & Ypres.	1 3/18		Usual routine	
	2 3/18		Attended conference at office of ADVS, 22nd Corps.	
	3 3/18	to 8/18	Usual routine	
"	9 3/18.		Conference at ADVS 22 Corps.	
"	10th to 11th		Usual routine	
"	12th		Capt. J. MARTIN. A.V.C joined division from No 12 VH in relief of Capt. R.S.L BEAUMONT. A.V.C struck off the strength as sick in England	
"	13th to 20th		Usual routine. A few cases of suspected Mange evacuated during this period.	
"	21st		Attended a conference at ABEELE DVS ADVS Corps & DADVS of divisions of 2nd Army present.	
"	22-26		Usual routine. DHQ shelled at intervals by a long range gun. 3 chargers & 6 wounded in DHQ stable.	

D. D. & L., London, E.C. (A8004) Wt. W1771/M2 31 750,000 5/17 Sch. 52 Forms/C2118/14

Instructions regarding War Diaries and Intelligence Summaries are contained in F. S. Regs., Part II. and the Staff Manual respectively. Title pages will be prepared in manuscript.

WAR DIARY
or
INTELLIGENCE SUMMARY.
(Erase heading not required.)

D.A D.V.S
37TH DIVISION

Army Form C. 2118.

Place	Date	Hour	Summary of Events and Information	Remarks and references to Appendices
ANZAC Camp	27.3.18		Received orders to entrain division. Division entrain at CAESTRE + HOPOUTRE. M.V.S from former DHQ from latter. DIV Arty + No 1 Coy Train remain behind. Left with DH.Q at 9.55 p.m + arrived at BOUQUET MAISON at 7.30. a.m on 28.3.18 Marched from there to TOUTENCOURT M.V.S arrived at 4.0 a.m on 29th. Marched from there to PAS. M.V.S located at FAMECHON. Under 4th Corps for administration.	
PAS	31.3.18		Remained here to date. Division taking over from 62 DIV.	
			37 DIV arrived in France on 1st August 1915	
			Lieut. Craig AVC granted 14 day leave from 22.3.18 Recalled on 24.3.18 by wire & had not rejoined at end of month.	
			J Henerson Major D.A D.V.S 37TH DIVISION	

19

Instructions regarding War Diaries and Intelligence Summaries are contained in F. S. Regs., Part II. and the Staff Manual respectively. Title pages will be prepared in manuscript.

WAR DIARY
or
INTELLIGENCE SUMMARY.
(Erase heading not required.)

D. A D. V. S
37TH DIVISION

Army Form C. 2118.

Vol 3

Place	Date	Hour	Summary of Events and Information	Remarks and references to Appendices
PAS	1.4.18		Visited units. 28 M.V.S located at FAMECHON. Advanced DHQ at SOUASTRE	JB
"	2.4.18		Usual routine	
COUIN	3.4.18		Advanced DHQ moved from SOUASTE + Rear DHQ from PAS to COUIN	
"	4.4.18		Visited M.V.S at FAMECHON. Received memo for O/c AVC Base Records requiring following information to be inserted in Diary. Date of Mobilisation of 37 DIV: was 4.4.15 28 M.V.S 37th DIV mobilised on 24.4.15 under command of Capt: Prior. A.V.C. + proceeded to BEF on 1.8.15 MAJOR J.R. STEEVENSON appointed ADVS of Division on 28 Aug: 1916 in succession to Major W.A. PALLIN A.V.C.	JB JB
"	4.4.18		Compiling returns. 41st DIV: Arty attached to 37 DIV for administration	JB
"	5.4.18		Infantry Bdes transport lines were heavily shelled. 15 mules ~~killed~~, 8 Riders + 2 H.D horses killed. 11 mules 2 Riders 4 HD horses + 1 LD horse wounded + sent to 28 M.V.S. 4 mules 2 Riders + 1 LD horse slightly wounded + remaining in lines.	JB

D. D. & L., London, E.C.
(A8004) Wt. W1771/M2 31 750,000 5/17 Sch. 52 Forms/C2118/14

Army Form C. 2118.

Instructions regarding War Diaries and Intelligence Summaries are contained in F. S. Regs., Part II. and the Staff Manual respectively. Title pages will be prepared in manuscript.

WAR DIARY
or
INTELLIGENCE SUMMARY.
(Erase heading not required.)

D.A.D.V.S
87TH DIVISION

Place	Date	Hour	Summary of Events and Information	Remarks and references to Appendices
GOUIN	6.4.18		Attended conference at office of ADVS 4th Corps. Visited 28 M.V.S at FAMECHON & afterwards accompanied Capt: J. Martin AVC to transport lines of Infty Bdes.	JS.
"	7.4.18		Visited transport lines & waggon lines of DIV Train. Received a wire stating that Capt: E P A. OFFORD A.V.C was posted to 37 Division in relief of Capt: J. Craig A.V.C sick in England. C/124 RFA rejoined division from 4th Army School	JS. JS.
"	8.4.18		Usual routine. Capt: E.P. OFFORD. A.V.C. arrived for duty in 37 DIVISION from No 2 Vety: Hospital.	
"	9.4.18		Visited 28 M.V.S & usual routine. 37th DIV Arty rejoined the division from 2nd Army. Saw ADVS 4th Corps in PAS. 2 animals killed & 4 wounded by shell fire. All belonging to Infty transport.	JS.
"	10.4.18		Inspected animals of 123 & 124 Bde RFA which arrived yesterday. Animals looking very fit. One horse only was left behind on the march from Belgium from the whole of the 37 DIV Arty which considering the march was done in 3 days is very good indeed. A few galls occurred & practically no shoes were lost during the march	JS.

D. D. & L., London, E.C. (A8004) Wt. W1771/M2 31 750,000 5/17 Sch. 52 Forms/C2118/14

Instructions regarding War Diaries and Intelligence Summaries are contained in F. S. Regs., Part II. and the Staff Manual respectively. Title pages will be prepared in manuscript.

WAR DIARY
or
INTELLIGENCE SUMMARY.
(Erase heading not required.)

Army Form C. 2118.

D. A. D. V. S
87TH DIVISION

Place	Date	Hour	Summary of Events and Information	Remarks and references to Appendices
COUIN.	11.4.18		Conference of V.O's i/c units. V.O's i/c 41 & 47 DIV: Artys attended as these units are attached to the Division. Compiling A.F.A.2000.	JS
"	12.4.18		28 M.V.S moved from FAMECHON to AUTIE ST. LEDGER this was done to make room for French troops in FAMECHON. Visited R.A. units. Despatched A F A 2000 to ADVS. 4th Corps.	JS.
"	13.4.18		Attended conference at office of ADVS 4th Corps. Visited 28 M.V.S & units of division. 28 M.V.S now entirely in the open as there is no cover available.	JS.
	14.4.18		Visited 37 DIV Train & M.V.S. Usual routine	JS
	15.4.18		Inspected remounts on arrival at PUCHEVILLERS station & distributed them to units. Usual routine. Received orders for D.H.Q to move to PAS on 16.4.18. M.V.S will not move.	JS.
AUTHIE	16.4.18		D.H.Q moved to AUTHIE instead of PAS. Usual routine	JS
"	17.4.18		~~Conference of V.O's i/c units.~~ Visited R.A waggon lines. & usual routine.	JS

D. D. & L., London, E.C.
(A8004) Wt. W1771/M2 31 750,000 5/17 Sch. 52 Forms/C2118/14

Army Form C. 2118.

WAR DIARY
or
INTELLIGENCE SUMMARY.
(Erase heading not required.)

Instructions regarding War Diaries and Intelligence Summaries are contained in F. S. Regs., Part II. and the Staff Manual respectively. Title pages will be prepared in manuscript.

D.A.D.V.S
37TH DIVISION

Place	Date	Hour	Summary of Events and Information	Remarks and references to Appendices
AUTHIE	18.4.18		41st & 44th Div. Artys which were attached to 37 DIV for administration were handed over to DADVS 42nd Division on relief on 16.4.18. Conference of VO's i/c units. A.D.V.S 4th Corps called at	J.S.
"			my office. Preparing A.F.A 2000 for week ending 18/4/18	J.S.
"	19.4.18.		Completed & despatched A F A 2000 to ADVS 4 Corps. 2nd M.V.S moved into billets in AUTHIE the weather being very inclement for horses in the open	J.S.
"	20.4.18		Attended conference at office of ADVS 4th Corps	J.S.
"	21.4.18		Usual routine.	
"	22.4.18.		Usual routine. Reported to ADVS 4th Corps that the Copra Cake issued as fodder in lieu of the 2 lbs of oats deducted from the normal ration was unsatisfactory as useless as a fodder as animals absolutely refused to eat it.	J.S.
"	23.4.18		Usual routine.	
HENU	24.4.18		D H Q. moved from AUTHIE to PAS. ADVS 4th Corps visited division & inspected some units	J.S.

D. D. & L., London, E.C.
(A8004) Wt. W1771/M2 31 750,000 5/17 Sch. 52 Forms/C2118/14

Instructions regarding War Diaries and Intelligence Summaries are contained in F. S. Regs., Part II. and the Staff Manual respectively. Title pages will be prepared in manuscript.

WAR DIARY
or
INTELLIGENCE SUMMARY.
(Erase heading not required.)

D.A.D.V.S
37TH DIVISION

Army Form C. 2118.

Place	Date	Hour	Summary of Events and Information	Remarks and references to Appendices
HENU	25.4.18		Conference of V.O's i/c units. Usual routine	[illegible]
"	26.4.18		Usual routine. Compiling AFA 2000. & despatched same to ADVS 4th Corps	[illegible]
"	27.4.18		Attended conference at office of ADVS 4th Corps. Visited units & usual routine	[illegible]
"	28.4.18		Usual routine	[illegible]
	29.4.18		59th Div Arty attached to me for administration	[illegible]
	30.4.18		Usual routine	

J. Stevenson
Major.

D.A.D.V.S
37TH DIVISION

D. D. & L., London, E.C.
(A8004) Wt. W1771/M2731 750,000 5/17 Sch. 52 Forms/C2118/14

11

Instructions regarding War Diaries and Intelligence Summaries are contained in F. S. Regs., Part II. and the Staff Manual respectively. Title pages will be prepared in manuscript.

WAR DIARY
or
INTELLIGENCE SUMMARY.
(Erase heading not required.)

Army Form C. 2118.

DADVS 37 D

Vol 34

Place	Date	Hour	Summary of Events and Information	Remarks and references to Appendices
HENU.	1.5.18		Usual routine. Visited transport lines	JS
"	2.5.18		Conference of V.O.'s i/c units including V.O.'s of 59th DIV: Arty attached	
"	3.5.18		Prepared ~~&~~ despatched AFA 2000 to ADVS 4th Corps.	
			Usual routine. Visited transport ~~lines~~ & lines of 296 Bde 59th DIV Arty. Animals of latter in bad condition & appear to want a great deal more attention.	JS
"	4.5.18		Attended conference at office of ADVS 4th Corps. Was informed that the establishment of vety. evacuation stations (1 per corps) had been improved. This entails the reduction of each mobile vety section by a Staff Sergeant & 6 men, which will leave the M.V.S. with barely sufficient men to carry on. It will also mean that fewer cases can be treated in M.V.S.s & returned direct to their units. These will a many of them be evacuated & so lost to the formation	JS JS JS
			Usual routine.	
"	5.5.18		Usual routine.	
	6.5.18		do do	JS

D. D. & L., London, E.C.
(A8004) Wt. W1771/M2-31 750,000 5/17 Sch. 52 Forms/C2118/14

Instructions regarding War Diaries and Intelligence Summaries are contained in F. S. Regs., Part II. and the Staff Manual respectively. Title pages will be prepared in manuscript.

WAR DIARY
or
INTELLIGENCE SUMMARY.
(Erase heading not required.)

D. A D. V. S
87TH DIVISION

Army Form C. 2118.

Place	Date	Hour	Summary of Events and Information	Remarks and references to Appendices
HENU	4.5.18		A.D.V.S 4th Corps visit all waggon lines of 37 DIV ARTY & afterwards sent a letter to the IV Corps Commander expressing himself as very pleased with the condition of the animals.	J.
"	8.5.18		Usual routine. One case of mustard gas poisoning occurred & was evacuated	J.
	9.5.18		Conference of V.O i/c units & office routine	J.
	10.5.18		Compiling A F A 2000. The 59th DIV Arty evacuated during week ending 10.5.18 34 cases of debility	J.
	11.5.18		Attended conference at office of A D V S 4th Corps. Usual routine.	J.
"	12.5.18		Usual routine. Inspected transport animals of 1/1 Herts Regt: which has just joined the division to replace 6th Bedfords transferred to a Cadre Division. The animals were not in good condition & shoeing was very bad. Reported this to Q & steps taken to have this remedied.	J.

D. D. & L., London, E.C.
(A8004) Wt. W1771/M2731 750,000 5/17 Sch. 52 Forms/C2118/14

Instructions regarding War Diaries and Intelligence Summaries are contained in F. S. Regs., Part II. and the Staff Manual respectively. Title pages will be prepared in manuscript.

WAR DIARY
or
INTELLIGENCE SUMMARY.
(Erase heading not required.)

Army Form C. 2118.

D. A. D. V. S
37TH DIVISION

Place	Date	Hour	Summary of Events and Information	Remarks and references to Appendices
HENU	13.5.18		Visited units & usual routine The IV Corps Commander under authority delegated to him awarded the following decoration to the undernamed No: SE 6928 Pte (A/Sgt) G.D.W. THOMAS A.V.C. Military Medal For conspicuous gallantry & devotion to duty near BAYENCOURT on 5th April 1918. (37th DIV. Routine Order No 3444 d 23.4.18) 37th DIV: Order No 2000 received. D.H.Q will move to AUTHIE at 4.0 p.m. on 17th May 1918.	JB.
	14.5.18		Usual routine	
	15.5.18		Col: W.A PALLIN. DDVS 3 Army visited division & inspected horses of 37 DIV: Train & 28 M.V.S.	JB.
	16.5.18		Conference of V.O's units & usual routine	2.
AUTHIE	17.5.18		D.H.Q moved to AUTHIE & division came out of the line being relieved by 62 DIVISION. Compiled & despatched AFA 2000 for week ending 16 May.	JB

D. D. & L., London, E.C. (A8004) Wt. W1771/M2731 750,000 5/17 Sch. 52 Forms/C2118/14

Instructions regarding War Diaries and Intelligence Summaries are contained in F. S. Regs., Part II. and the Staff Manual respectively. Title pages will be prepared in manuscript.

WAR DIARY
or
INTELLIGENCE SUMMARY.
(Erase heading not required.)

D.A D.V.S
87TH DIVISION

Army Form C. 2118.

Place	Date	Hour	Summary of Events and Information	Remarks and references to Appendices
AUTHIE	18.5.18		Attended at office of ADVS 4th Corps & afterwards visited No 14 Vety Hospital at ABBEVILLE	[illegible]
	19.5.18		Inspected transport animals of 63rd & 111th Infty Bdes. Despatched copy of AFA 2000 for 59th Div Arty to DADVS 62 Division as they are now under his administration.	[illegible]
	20.5.18 to 22.5.18		Usual routine.	[illegible]
	23.5.18		Conference of V.O. i/c units & usual routine.	[illegible]
	24.5.18		Prepared & despatched A.FA 2000 to A.D.V.S IV Corps.	[illegible]
	25.5.18		Attended conference at office of ADVS. IV. Corps & usual routine	[illegible]
	26 to 28.5.18		Usual routine, nothing of importance to record. 6 men despatched from 28 M.V.S to join No 4 V.E.S which is established at AUTHIEULE.	[illegible]
	29.5.18		Usual routine	
	30.5.18		Conference of V.O. i/c units.	
	31.5.18		Prepared & despatched AFA 2000 to ADVS 4th Corps	

[illegible signature]
Major
D.A.D.V.S
87TH DIVISION

D. D. & L., London, E.C. (A8004) Wt. W1771/M2031 750,000 5/17 Sch. 52 Forms/C2118/14

17

Instructions regarding War Diaries and Intelligence Summaries are contained in F. S. Regs., Part II. and the Staff Manual respectively. Title pages will be prepared in manuscript.

WAR DIARY
or
INTELLIGENCE SUMMARY.

(Erase heading not required.)

Army Form C. 2118.

D.A.D.V.S
37TH DIVISION

33

Place	Date	Hour	Summary of Events and Information	Remarks and references to Appendices
AUTHIE	1.6.18		Attended conference at office of ADVS IV Corps. Usual routine. Division placed in G H Q reserve	
	2.6.18 3.6.18		Usual routine	
	4.6.18		Divisional transport competition	
	5.6.18		D.H.Q moved to CAVILLON. Transport by road, remainder by bus. Transferred to XXII Corps Fourth Army	
CAVILLON	6.6.18		Went round the area. DDMVS at BREILLY. Reported arrival to ADVS XXII Corps & asked for information re evacuation of sick animals.	
	7.6.18		Reported to ADVS 22 Corps at MOLLIENS VIDAME	
	8.6.18 9.6.18		Visited units. Usual routine. Two animals were left behind on the march down from AUTHIE by the DIV ARTY taken into British units & were evacuated sick.	
WAILLY	10.6.18 to 18.6.18		D H Q moved to WAILLY on 10th inst. Division in reserve to 9th French Corps. MVS at PLACHY-BUYON. Nothing of importance in the way of sickness or inefficiency amongst the animals. Received from DDVS 3rd Army an extract from his report to 3rd Army stating that the transport of 37 DIV: was in every way the best that was seen in the 3rd Army	

D. D. & L., London, E.C. (A8004). Wt. W1771/M2 31 750,000 5/17 Sch. 52 Forms/C2118/14

Instructions regarding War Diaries and Intelligence Summaries are contained in F. S. Regs., Part II. and the Staff Manual respectively. Title pages will be prepared in manuscript.

WAR DIARY
or
INTELLIGENCE SUMMARY.
(Erase heading not required.)

D.A.D.V.S 37TH DIVISION

Army Form C. 2118.

Place	Date	Hour	Summary of Events and Information	Remarks and references to Appendices
WAILLY	19.6.18.		Usual routine. Division ordered to join 4th Corps 3rd Army. Transport by road & Personnel by tactical train.	JH
"	20.6.18		Transport left by road for PAS area. Two days march.	
PAS	21.6.18		DHQ & Division arrived in PAS area. Two horses left behind on march, one Kick & one PUN	JH
"	22.6.18		Attended conference at office of ADVS 4th Corp.	JH
"	23.6.18 / 24.6.18		Usual routine. 28 M.V.S located at PAS	JH
	25.6.18		Conference of V.O's	JH
	26.6.18		Preparing & despatched AFA 2000. Usual routine	
	27.6.18		Attended conference at office of ADVS IV Corp.	JH
	28.6.18 / 30.6.18		Usual routine.	JH

J. Harrison [signature]
Major
D.A.D.V.S 37TH DIVISION

D. D. & L., London, E.C. (A8004) Wt. W1771/M2-31 750,000 5/17 Sch. 52 Forms/C2118/14

19

Instructions regarding War Diaries and Intelligence Summaries are contained in F. S. Regs., Part II. and the Staff Manual respectively. Title pages will be prepared in manuscript.

WAR DIARY
or
INTELLIGENCE SUMMARY.
(Erase heading not required.)

Army Form C. 2118.

D.A D.V.S
37TH DIVISION

VIII 36

Place	Date	Hour	Summary of Events and Information	Remarks and references to Appendices
PAS	1.VII.18 to 3.VII.18		Usual routine. Inspection of transport of units	
"	4.VII.18		Conference of V.Os in my office.	
"	5.VII.18		Prepared & dispatched AFA2000 to ADVS 4th Corps	
"	6.VII.18		Attended conference at office of ADVS 4th Corps	
"	7.VII.18 8.VII.18		Usual routine. On 8.VII.18 14 horses of B/123/RFA were killed by shell fire & 4 horses wounded.	
"	9.VII.18		Went to see ADVS 4th Corps with a view to taking over his duties whilst he is on leave to England. Arranged to take over on 10th inst.	
"	10.VII.18 to 24.VII.18		Acted as ADVS IV Corps during absence on leave of Lt. Col. C B M Harris DSO. Capt. J.H. Yates AVC OC 25 MVS went on leave on 20th inst.	
"	25.VII.18		Capt. J. Martin AVC to act as O.C MVS during his absence	
"	31.VII.18		Usual routine. Nothing of note to record.	

[illegible] Major
D.A D.V.S
37TH DIVISION

D. D. & L., London, E.C. (A8004) Wt. W1771/M2-31 750,000 5/17 Sch. 52 Forms/C2118/14

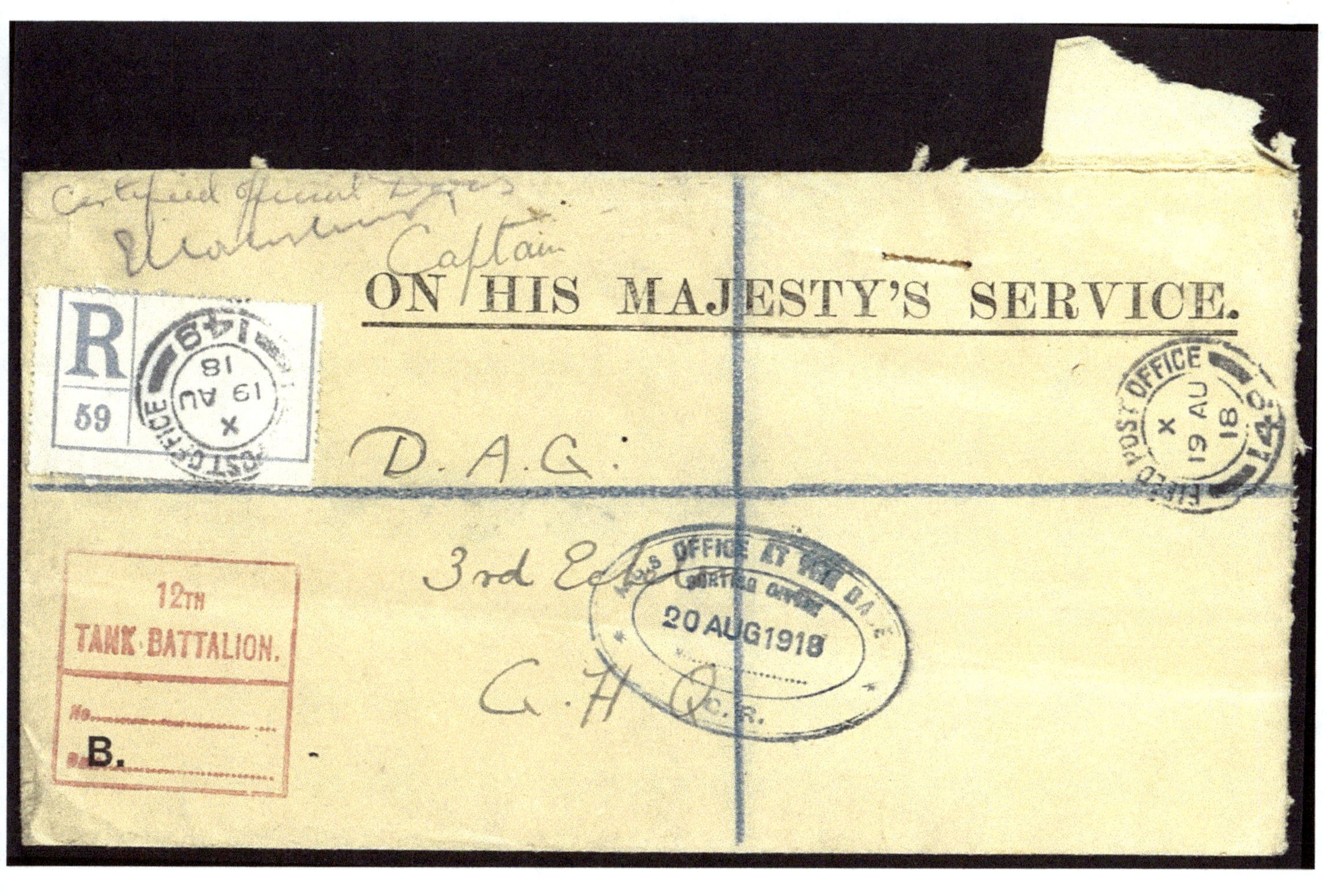

Captain
ON HIS MAJESTY'S SERVICE.
R
59
19 AU 18
FIELD POST OFFICE
D.A.G.
3rd Ech.
G.H.Q.
20 AUG 1918
12TH
TANK BATTALION.
No.
B.

8

Army Form C. 2118.

D.A.D.V.S
37TH DIVISION

WAR DIARY
or
INTELLIGENCE SUMMARY.
(*Erase heading not required.*)

Instructions regarding War Diaries and Intelligence Summaries are contained in F. S. Regs., Part II. and the Staff Manual respectively. Title pages will be prepared in manuscript.

VR 37

Place	Date	Hour	Summary of Events and Information	Remarks and references to Appendices
HENU	1.8.18		Visited transport lines, & routine	JH
	2.8.18		do do Despatched AFA 2000.	J
"	3.8.18		Attended conference at office of ADVS IV Corps. Routine.	
"	4.8.18 to 9.8.18		29 Canadian Forestry Coy: attached for vety administration. Usual routine & inspection of transport & waggon lines of units in the division	J
	10.8.18		Attended conference at office of ADVS IV Corps.	JH
	11.8.18 to 16.8.18		Usual routine. 1 case of suspected mange evacuated from 153 Field Coy R.E. otherwise no contagious disease of any importance except Opthalmia of which there are about 20 cases under treatment	JH
"	17.8.18		Conference at office of ADVS IV Corps.	JH
"	18.8.18		Usual routine.	
"	19.8.18		Major J. R. Stevenson A.V.C left on leave to England for fourteen days Capt. J. Martin A.V.C (T.F) is performing his duties.	JH / J
	20.8.18 to 22.8.18		Usual routine. Inspection of transport lines of Units of Division	JM

D. D. & L., London, E.C. (A8004) Wt. W1771/M2031 750,000 5/17 Sch. 52 Forms/C2118/14

Instructions regarding War Diaries and Intelligence Summaries are contained in F. S. Regs., Part II. and the Staff Manual respectively. Title pages will be prepared in manuscript.

WAR DIARY
or
INTELLIGENCE SUMMARY.
(Erase heading not required.)

D.A.D.V.S 37TH DIVISION

Army Form C. 2118.

Place	Date	Hour	Summary of Events and Information	Remarks and references to Appendices
HENU	22/8/18		Usual routine. Conference of V.O.s Advanced collecting post fixed at 38 Souastre.	JM
	23/8/18		Inspection of 112 Brigade and RE companies. Despatched A.2000 to Corps. Major Connell arrived this evening and took over duties of DADVS during absence of Major Stevenson on leave.	JM.
"	24/8/18		Conference at office of A D V S IV Corps. Reported to G O C 37th Div at advanced Div Hd Qrs at Fonquevillers	JAC
	25/8/18		Move from Henu to FONQUEVILLERS	JAC
Fonquevillers	26/8/18		Move of 28th M.V.S. from PAS to FONQUEVILLERS advanced collecting post at SOUASTRE closed.	JAC
FONQUEVILLERS	27/8/18		28th M.V.S moved to LOGEAST WOOD Sheet 57D F 30 Central Inspected Waggon lines of 111th Inf Bde.	JAC
"	28/8/18		Inspected Horse lines of Div Train	JAC
"	29/8/18		Usual routine, inspected waggon lines D.A.C. Conference of V.O.s	JAC
"	30/8/18		Usual routine, despatched A.F.A 2000 to IV Corps	JAC
"	31/8/18		Move from FONQUEVILLERS to ACHIET-LE-GRAND. Inspected Remounts at Beaucourt.	J.A. Connell JAC

D. D. & L., London, E.C. (A8004) Wt. W1771/M2 31 750,000 5/17 Sch. 52 Forms/C2118/14

D.A.D.V.S 37TH DIVISION

21

Instructions regarding War Diaries and Intelligence Summaries are contained in F. S. Regs., Part II. and the Staff Manual respectively. Title pages will be prepared in manuscript.

WAR DIARY
or
INTELLIGENCE SUMMARY.
(Erase heading not required.)

D.A.D.V.S
37TH DIVISION

Army Form C. 2118.

Vol 38

Place	Date	Hour	Summary of Events and Information	Remarks and references to Appendices
ACHIET-LE-GRAND	1 Sept		Inspection of Waggon lines of No 3 Section D.A.C.	
Do	2		Inspection of Waggon lines of B. C & D Batteries 124th Bde R.F.A.	
Do	3		Inspection of ~~...~~ Hd Qrs & Signal Co Transport lines of 112th Inf Bde & No 2 Section D.A.C.	
Do	4		Usual Routine	
Do	5		Conference with V.O's	
Do	6		Meeting Remounts at Achiet-le-Grand station. despatched a 2000's	
Do	7		Conference at IV Corps.	
Do	8		Move from ACHIET-LE-GRAND to FAVREUIL.	
FAVREUIL	9 & 10		Inspection of Waggon lines of A Battery 124th Bde R.F.A. & A. C & D Batteries 123rd Bde R.F.A.	
Do	11		Inspection of Waggon lines of 152. 153 & 154 Field Co R.E. Move to J 36. D 9.1. Move of 28th Mobile Vet Section from FAVREUIL to FREMICOURT.	
J 36 D 9.1 Ref Map 57 C.	12		Conference with V.O. advanced collecting post established at P.1.C.7.3.	
Do	13		Collecting Remounts at ACHIET-LE-GRAND.	
Do	14		Conference at A.D.V.S. IV Corps. Inspection of Waggon lines of 317th Bde R.F.A. & No 2 Section D.A.C. 63rd Div attached.	
Do	15		Inspecting mange infected Stables ~~at~~ in Divisional new area.	

D. D. & L., London, E.C. (A8004) Wt. W1771/M2 31 750,000 5/17 Sch. 52 Forms/C2118/14

Instructions regarding War Diaries and Intelligence Summaries are contained in F. S. Regs., Part II. and the Staff Manual respectively. Title pages will be prepared in manuscript.

WAR DIARY
or
INTELLIGENCE SUMMARY.
(*Erase heading not required.*)

Army Form C. 2118.

D.A D.V.S. 37TH DIVISION

Place	Date	Hour	Summary of Events and Information	Remarks and references to Appendices
I 26 d 9.1.	Sept 16		Inspecting Transport Lines of 63rd Inf Bde	
Do	"		Inspecting B Battery Waggon Lines 123 Bde R.F.A. + No 1 Sec D.A.C.	
Do	17		Inspection of Transport Lines of 37th Machine Gun Btn.	
Do	18		Inspection of Transport Lines of 111th Inf Bde.	
Do	19		Inspections of Transport Lines of 48th + 49th Field Ambulance.	
"	"		Conference with V.O.s at this office.	
			MAJOR T. R STEEVENSON returned from leave to England	
Velu	20th		Visited units.	
ACHIET le GRAND.	21st		Attended conference at A.D.V.S IV Corps at GREVILLERS.	
			M.V.S moved from Fremicourt to WARLENCOURT EAUCOURT.	
			DHQ moved to ACHIET le GRAND.	[illegible]
"	22nd 23 24 25		Usual routine 37 Div Arty attached to 42 Div & infantry at rest in THILLOY, WARLENCOURT. PYS area. Artillery have heavy casualties from shell fire	
	26		Conference of V.Os.	
	27		Preparing A.F.A 2000 & usual routine	

D. D. & L., London, E.C. (A8004) Wt. W1771/M2 31 750,000 5/17 Sch. 52 Forms/C2118/14

Instructions regarding War Diaries and Intelligence Summaries are contained in F. S. Regs., Part II. and the Staff Manual respectively. Title pages will be prepared in manuscript.

WAR DIARY
or
INTELLIGENCE SUMMARY.

(Erase heading not required.)

Army Form C. 2118.

D.A D.V.S
37TH DIVISION

Place	Date	Hour	Summary of Events and Information	Remarks and references to Appendices
ACHIET LE GRAND	28.9.18.		DDVS 3rd Army visited DHQ + took Major Connell AVC to 42nd DIV on his appointment there as DADVS.	
			attended conference with ADVS 4 Corps.	
"			No 4 VES ordered to move to YTRES railhead.	
"	29.9.18		DH.Q moved to VILLERS AU FLOS + also 28 M.V.S to same place	
VILLERS AU FLOS	30.9.18		DH.Q moved to P 18 d (Sheet 57c) in HAVRINCOURT Wood about a mile N of METZ en COUTURE. 28 M.V.S to NEUVILLE BOURJONVAL Division took over line from 5th Division.	

[illegible signature]
Major

D.A.D.V.S
37TH DIVISION

D. D. & L., London, E.C.
(A8004) Wt. W1771/M2031 750,000 5/17 Sch. 52 Forms/C2118/14

3

Instructions regarding War Diaries and Intelligence Summaries are contained in F. S. Regs., Part II. and the Staff Manual respectively. Title pages will be prepared in manuscript.

WAR DIARY
or
INTELLIGENCE SUMMARY.
(Erase heading not required.)

Army Form C. 2118.

D.A.D.V.S
37TH DIVISION

Vol 40

Place	Date	Hour	Summary of Events and Information	Remarks and references to Appendices
HAVRINCOURT Wood (P 15 d) Sheet 57 C)	1.10.18		Visited units. Some horses falling off in condition as a result of work during operations.	
	2.10.18		do do	H.
	3.10.18		Conference of V.Os. Divl. Arty lost 89 horses killed & destroyed as a result of bomb & shell fire & 34 evacuated wounded during week ending 3.10.18. 223 Bde R.F.A 63rd Division attached for administration	H. H.
"	4.10.18		Visited units. 111th Infy Bde transport animals too crowded & likely to draw fire. G.O.C gave instructions for them to be moved & spread out more	
"	5.10.18		Conference at office ADVS IV Corps at No 4 V.E.S at Ytres. Advanced D.H.Q moved to Q 29 a.	H
"	6.10.18		Capt. E.A.P. Offord AVC V.O. i/c 37 DIV Train proceeded on leave in lieu sick leave from Boulogne to England from 6.10.18 to 19.10.18. 28 M.V.S moved to GOUZEAUCOURT.	
Q 29 Central Sheet 57 C	7.10.18		Rear D.H.Q with myself moved to Q.29. Central. Advanced DHQ to Bois Lateau.	H.

D. D. & L., London, E.C. (A8004) Wt. W1771/M231 750,000 5/17 Sch. 52 Forms/C2118/14

Instructions regarding War Diaries and Intelligence Summaries are contained in F. S. Regs., Part II. and the Staff Manual respectively. Title pages will be prepared in manuscript.

WAR DIARY
or
INTELLIGENCE SUMMARY.
(Erase heading not required.)

Army Form C. 2118.

D. A. D. V. S
37TH DIVISION

Place	Date	Hour	Summary of Events and Information	Remarks and references to Appendices
Q 29 Central.	8.10.18		37 Div Arty had 34 animals killed or destroyed from shell fire or bombs 14 evacuated to M.V.S + 29 wounded remaining in lines in 24 hours ending 12 p.m. 8.10.18	
	9.10.18		28 M.V.S moved to VAUCELLES M.15 d (Sheet 57 b).	[initials]
HAUCOURT	10.10.18		D.H.Q moved to HAUCOURT + 28 M.V.S to Chateau BRISEUX	[initials]
"	11.10.18		Usual routine.	[initials]
"	12.10.18		Visited units.	
"	13.10.18		28 M.V.S moved to LIGNY en CAMBRESIS. IV Corps H Q moved to LIGNY	
"	14.10.18		Visited units.	
"	15.10.18		Opened 37 Div Clipping Station at LIGNY. 74 horses clipped. This station is under the direction of Capt. J. H. Yates O.C 28 M.V.S.	[initials]
"	16.10.18		Visited units - Conference at Office of A.D.V.S IV Corps.	
"	19.10.18		100 odd horses being clipped daily at clipping station	[initials]
"	20 to 22 10.18		Visited units nothing of importance to record.	[initials]
"	23.10.18		D.H.Q moved to BRIASTRE.	
"	24.10.18		28 M.V.S moved to CAUDRY. Also Clipping Station to same place.	

D. D. & L., London, E.C.
(A8004) Wt. W1771/M2631 750,000 5/17 Sch. 52 Forms/C2118/14

Instructions regarding War Diaries and Intelligence Summaries are contained in F. S. Regs., Part II. and the Staff Manual respectively. Title pages will be prepared in manuscript.

WAR DIARY
or
INTELLIGENCE SUMMARY.
(Erase heading not required.)

Army Form C. 2118.

D.A.D.V.S
37TH DIVISION

Place	Date	Hour	Summary of Events and Information	Remarks and references to Appendices
BRIASTRE	25.10.18		28 M.V.S to BEAURAIN. & Clipping Station to BRIASTRE. Clipping finished for Infantry Bdes & Train. All these clipped out. Div Arty being clipped trace high only	
"	26.10.18 to 31.10.18		Visiting units & [illegible]. Nothing of note to record.	

J. [illegible]
Major
D.A.D.V.S
37TH DIVISION

D. D. & L., London, E.C.
(A8004) Wt. W1771/M2 31 750,000 5/17 Sch. 52 Forms/C2118/14

4

Instructions regarding War Diaries and Intelligence Summaries are contained in F. S. Regs., Part II. and the Staff Manual respectively. Title pages will be prepared in manuscript.

WAR DIARY
or
INTELLIGENCE SUMMARY.
(Erase heading not required.)

Army Form C. 2118.

D.A.D.V.S 37TH DIVISION

Vol 41

Place	Date	Hour	Summary of Events and Information	Remarks and references to Appendices
BRIASTRE	1.11.18 to 5.11.18		Inspection of units. Usual routine.	H
NEUVILLE	6.11.18		D.H.Q moved to NEUVILLE. 28 M.V.S to LOUVIGNIES	H
"	to 10.11.18		Also clipping establishment. Usual routine.	H
CAUDRY	11.11.18		D.H.Q & 28 M.V.S & Clipping estab. moved back to Caudry. Hostilities ceased at 11.0 a.m. Division in Caudry, Bethencourt & VIESLY	H.
"	19.11.18		Inspected 298 Army Field Arty Bde which is now attached to division. Capt: Mellett. AVC is V.O. i/c Capt. J. Martin proceeded on 14 days leave	H. H
"	20.11.18 to 30.11.18		Usual routine. 1 case of suspected mange evacuated from D/123/RFA.	

J Hueman [illegible]
Major

D.A.D.V.S 37TH DIVISION

D. D. & L., London, E.C. (A8004) Wt. W1771/M2-31 750,000 5/17 Sch. 52 Forms/C2118/14

1/2

Army Form C. 2118.

DADVS 37 D

Vol 42

WAR DIARY
or
INTELLIGENCE SUMMARY.
(Erase heading not required.)

Instructions regarding War Diaries and Intelligence Summaries are contained in F. S. Regs., Part II. and the Staff Manual respectively. Title pages will be prepared in manuscript.

Place	Date	Hour	Summary of Events and Information	Remarks and references to Appendices
~~[illegible]~~ Caudry	1.12.18		Usual routine	JS
	2.12.18		DHQ moved to GOMMEGNIES. E of LE QUESNOY. also 28 M.V.S Div: Arty remaining at Caudry.	
GOMMEGNIES	3.12.18 to 9.12.18		nothing to record of importance. Capt. J. MARTIN A.V.C returned from leave on 6.12.18. On 9.12.18 visited DIV Arty + 298 Bde AFA to select mares for breeding purposes as ordered by 37 DIV Q.	JS
"	10.12.18 13.12.18		Usual routine. Visited units	
"	14.12.18		Capt: J.A McMenamin R.A.V.C joined division from HQ 2nd Army to take over duties of DADVS. 37 DIV	JS
Sous le Bois	15.12.18		D.H.Q + 28 M.V.S moved to SOUS le BOIS near MAUBERGE	JS
	16/17		Halted. Capt. OFFORD AVC granted 14 days special leave for boat sailing 20.12.18	
"	18.12.18		DHQ + 28 MVS marched to BINCHES	
"	19.12.18		Halted. Handed over duties of DADVS to Capt J. A. McMenamin + Major J. R. STEEVENSON leaves to assume duties of ADVS XI Corps on 21.12.18.	JS

D. D. & L., London, E.C. (A8004) Wt. W1771/M2931 750,000 5/17 Sch. 52 Forms/C2118/14

Instructions regarding War Diaries and Intelligence Summaries are contained in F. S. Regs., Part II. and the Staff Manual respectively. Title pages will be prepared in manuscript.

WAR DIARY
or
INTELLIGENCE SUMMARY.
(Erase heading not required.)

Army Form C. 2118.

Place	Date	Hour	Summary of Events and Information	Remarks and references to Appendices
Gosselies	20/12/18		D.H.Q & 28 M.V.S. moved from Binche to Gosselies	
do	21/12/18		Halted. Despatched A.F.A 2000 to A.D.V.S IV Corps	
do	22/12/18		Inspected units of 63 Inf Bde	
do	23/12/18		Inspected A & B/298 Bdes. condition of animals only fair, showing fair wastage of forage in B Battery noticeable. all animals dirty & unclipped.	
do	24/12/18		Inspected C & D/298 Bde. same remarks apply as to condition, also to the state of the coats. six cases of mange occurred. advised clipping of all animals in Bde.	
do	26/12/18		Inspected B.A.C. 298 Bde. condition of animals good with three exceptions coats dirty & unclipped. Chaff not being used in oat feeds.	
do	27/12/18		Inspected units of 112 Inf Bde	
do	28/12/18		Inspected units. Despatched A 2000 to A.D.V.S IV Corps.	
do	29/12/18		Inspected units	
do	30/12/18		Inspected units of 111 Inf Bde	
do	31/12/18		Inspected units	

J. McMenamin Major RAVC

D.A.D.V.S
37TH DIVISION

9/3

Instructions regarding War Diaries and Intelligence Summaries are contained in F. S. Regs., Part II. and the Staff Manual respectively. Title pages will be prepared in manuscript.

WAR DIARY
or
INTELLIGENCE SUMMARY.
(Erase heading not required.)

D.A.D.V.S
37TH DIVISION

37

Army Form C. 2118.

VIII 43

Place	Date	Hour	Summary of Events and Information	Remarks and references to Appendices
Gosnelies	1/1/19		Held the first Board on the classification of animals for purposes of demobilisation. Board comprised of Major J.A. McMeekin RAVC as President. Captains J.H. Yates & J. Martin both of RAVC as members. All animals in Div H.Q were inspected by the Board & classified	
	2/1/19		The above Board of Officers inspected the animals in charge of H.Q. Signals, Police & Area Employment Coy.	
	3/1/19		Board was held on animals of the D.A.C	
	4/1/19		Board held on Div units	
	5/1/19		do	
	6/1/19		do Capt Offord reported back from leave.	
	7/1/19		do	
	8/1/19		do	
	9/1/19		do	
	10/1/19		do	
	11/1/19		do	
	12/1/19		do	
	13/1/19		Board classified animals of 298 Bde R.F.A.	
	14/1/19		Board completed classification of animals 298 Bde R.F.A.	
	15/1/19		Board completed classification of the remaining animals in the Division.	
	16/1/19		Capt Yates proceeds on 14 days leave to England. D.A.D.V.S. acts as O/C M.V.S	
	17/1/19		usual routine	

A5834 Wt. W4973/M687 750,000 8/16 D. D. & L. Ltd. Forms/C.2118/13.

Instructions regarding War Diaries and Intelligence Summaries are contained in F. S. Regs., Part II. and the Staff Manual respectively. Title pages will be prepared in manuscript.

WAR DIARY
or
INTELLIGENCE SUMMARY.
(Erase heading not required.)

D.A.D.V.S
37TH DIVISION

Army Form C. 2118.

Place	Date	Hour	Summary of Events and Information	Remarks and references to Appendices
Gosselies	18/1/19		visited units	
	19/1/19		usual Routine.	
	20/1/19		do	
	21/1/19		do	
	22/1/19		do V.E.S & advanced Vety Hospital closed for reception of sick animals.	
	23/1/19		do	
	24/1/19		do	
	25/1/19		do	
	26/1/19		do	
	27/1/19		do	
	28/1/19		do Capt Willet RAVC reported for duty with 298 Bde R.F.A.	
	29/1/19		do commenced the malleining of all "Y" and "Z" animals. A camp for purposes of demobilisation of horses opened. Capt Willet appointed as V.O.i/c.	
	30/1/19		usual routine. lack of grooming noticeable amongst the animals of nearly all units visited due to the demobilisation of trained personnel.	
	31/1/19		usual Routine.	[signature]

31

D.A.D.V.S
37TH DIVISION Army Form C. 2118.

Instructions regarding War Diaries and Intelligence Summaries are contained in F. S. Regs., Part II. and the Staff Manual respectively. Title pages will be prepared in manuscript.

WAR DIARY
or
INTELLIGENCE SUMMARY.
(Erase heading not required.)

Vol 44

Place	Date	Hour	Summary of Events and Information	Remarks and references to Appendices
Gosselies	1/2/19		Usual Routine. Mallerining of animals proceeding	
	2/2/19		Capt Yates reported back from leave	
	3/2/19		Commenced the "setting apart" of "Z" animals not up to the standard required by the Belgian Government.	
	4/2/19		Fifty two brood mares sent by rail from Charleroi to Dieppe for repatriation to England.	
	5/2/19		about 336 animals have been "set apart" and are now marked "ZV"	
	6/2/19		usual routine	
	7/2/19		do	
	10/2/19		Sixty (60) "ZV" animals sent to IV V.E.S. for sale	
	12/2/19		one hundred & fifty two (152) "Y" animals were sent to Havre for repatriation to England	
	15/2/19		one hundred & forty four (144) "Y" animals sent to Havre for repatriation. Received authority for sale of "Z" animals & arranged for sales to take place at Gosselies on 19th & 22nd inst. 100 animals each day.	
	16/2/19		usual routine	
	17/2/19			
	18/2/19		144 Y animals sent to Base for repatriation	
	19/2/19		Sold seventy six (76) at sale of "Z" animals, 24 withdrawn — insufficient offer	JMitchell
	20/2/19		usual routine	

A5834 Wt. W4973/M687 500,000 8/16 D. D. & L. Ltd. Forms/C.2118/13.

Instructions regarding War Diaries and Intelligence Summaries are contained in F. S. Regs., Part II. and the Staff Manual respectively. Title pages will be prepared in manuscript.

WAR DIARY
or
INTELLIGENCE SUMMARY.
(Erase heading not required.)

D.V.D.V. 87TH DIVISION

Army Form C. 2118.

Place	Date	Hour	Summary of Events and Information	Remarks and references to Appendices
Gosselies	21/2/19		144 Y animals sent to base	
"	22/2/19		Sale of 'Z' animals at Gosselies sold 128, withdrawn 4	
	23/2/19		arranging concentration of animals for sale	
	24/2/19		Inspection of 200 Y animals for repatriation. sale of 126 Z animals 15 withdrawn	
	25/2/19		arranging concentration. branding of Z animals for sale next day.	
	26/2/19		Sale of 129 Z animals	
	27/2/19		arranging concentration of animals for sale. 150 Y animals inspected at railhead for repatriation	
	28/2/19		Sale of 150 'Z' animals, sold 117. Total amt realised 76,375 francs.	J.H.Mott

A5834 Wt. W4973/M687 750,000 8/16 D. D. & L. Ltd. Forms/C.2118/13.

Instructions regarding War Diaries and Intelligence Summaries are contained in F. S. Regs., Part II. and the Staff Manual respectively. Title pages will be prepared in manuscript.

24

WAR DIARY
or
INTELLIGENCE SUMMARY.
(Erase heading not required.)

D.A.D.V.S
37TH DIVISION

Army Form C. 2118.

Vol 45

Place	Date	Hour	Summary of Events and Information	Remarks and references to Appendices
Gosselies	1/3/19		Inspection of horses selected as Infantry chargers	
	2/3/19		Concentration of "Z" animals for sale, branding etc.	
	3/3/19		Sale of 98 "Z" horses & 24 "Z" mules. Total amt realised 74,585 Frs	
	4/3/19		Concentration of 170 "Z" animals for sale	
	5/3/19		Sale of 163 "Z" animals at Gosselies, average price for all classes 819 francs	
	6/3/19		~~Eight~~ Concentration of Z horses for sale	
	7/3/19		Eighth sale of Z animals, sold 106 horses & 51 mules Total amount realised francs 132,865.	
	8/3/19		usual routine	
	9/3/19		Concentration of animals for sale	
	10/3/19		Sale of 105 Z animals Total amt realised 96,700 francs	
	11/3/19		Concentration of Z animals for sale	
	12/3/19		Tenth & last sale of Z animals, 47 sold Total amount realised 47,660 francs.	
	13/3/19		usual routine	
	14/3/19		Selection of Infantry chargers	
	15/3/19		Transfer of 700 X animals to 123 & 124 Art Bdes	

A5834 Wt. W4973/M687 750,000 8/16 D. D. & L. Ltd. Forms/C.2118/13.

Instructions regarding War Diaries and Intelligence Summaries are contained in F. S. Regs., Part II. and the Staff Manual respectively. Title pages will be prepared in manuscript.

WAR DIARY
or
INTELLIGENCE SUMMARY.
(Erase heading not required.)

D.A.D.V.S
37TH DIVISION

Army Form C. 2118.

Place	Date	Hour	Summary of Events and Information	Remarks and references to Appendices
Gosselies	16/3/19		usual routine & inspection of 78 horses from 11th Canadian Forestry Co	
	17/3/19		S. S. horses dispatched to No 2 Remount Depot Havre	J. A. Neill
	18/3/19		Granted leave to Ireland & proceeding by Cologne express today. Capt Martin RAVC acting in my absence.	
	19/3/19		Commenced duties as acting DADVS during absence of Major McNamara	
	20/3/19		Usual routine. Weekly conference of V. O's.	
	21/3/19		Usual routine. A 2000 to Army.	
	22/3/19		Usual routine. Inspected animals of 37 L of Battalion.	
	23/3/19		Inspected 96 X animals proceeding to Havre.	
	24/3/19		Sale of 862 animals. Inspected 35 animals transferred from other units to complete L of Battalion. Inspected 96 X horses for Havre.	
	25/3/19		Usual routine.	
	26/3/19		Usual routine. Visited L of Battalion and Supply C.	
	27/3/19		Usual routine. Conference of V. O's	
	28/3/19		Usual routine. A 2000 to 4th Army.	
	29/3/19		Usual routine.	
	30/3/19		Inspected and entrained 152 X animals for Antwerp	
	31/3/19		Inspected and entrained 64 X animals for Antwerp.	J Martin

A5834 Wt. W4973/M687 750,000 8/16 D. D. & L. Ltd. Forms/C.2118/13.

Instructions regarding War Diaries and Intelligence Summaries are contained in F. S. Regs., Part II. and the Staff Manual respectively. Title pages will be prepared in manuscript.

24

WAR DIARY
or
INTELLIGENCE SUMMARY.
(Erase heading not required.)

D.A.D.V.S
37TH DIVISION

Army Form C. 2118.

46

Place	Date	Hour	Summary of Events and Information	Remarks and references to Appendices
Fosseles	1 April 19		Inspected and despatched 54 x animals to 5 Horse Con. Camp Nivelles.	
	2/4/19		Inspected and entrained 257 x animals for Remounts.	
	3/4/19		Usual routine. Conference of V. Os.	
	4/4/19		A 2000 to 4th Army. Major McKeown returned from leave and assumed duties of D.A.D.V.S	
	5/4/19			J Martin
	6/4/19		Capt Willet V.O. 298 Bde reported to concentration camp for demobilisation	
	7/4/19		Capts Martin & Offord left Division for demobilisation	
	9/4/19		Inspected 44 animals transferred to IV Corps H.A.	
	10/4/19		Inspected 63 & 111th Bde animals transferred to IV Corps H.A.	
	11/4/19		Inspected Train animals transferred to IV Corps H.A.	
	12/4/19		Inspected Div Arty animals transferred to No 11 Remount Squadron	
	14/4/19		Inspected Div ~~Arty~~ Field Ambulance animals transferred to Namur.	
	15/4/19		Inspected Div Field Ambulance animals transferred to Namur. Received instructions to take over duties as V.O. i/c Brabant area.	J Mc K
	16/4/19		Only 68 animals remaining	
	17/4/19		Capt Spurr started for England on duty.	
	18/4/19		Inspected remaining animals N. Staffs transferred to Essex Regt	
	19/4/19		37 Div Cadres left for England	J Mc K
	21/4/19			

A5834 Wt. W4973/M687 750,000 8/16 D. D. & L. Ltd. Forms/C.2118/13.

www.ingramcontent.com/pod-product-compliance
Lightning Source LLC
Chambersburg PA
CBHW081528160426
43191CB00011B/1707
* 9 7 8 1 4 7 4 5 1 8 0 7 9 *